Kerala Road Atlas
& STATE DISTANCE GUIDE

Edition - 2013

Editors :
Dr. R. P. Arya
Jitender Arya
Dr. Gayathri Arya
Anshuman Arya
Kanika Arya

CONTENTS

TITLE	PAGE
India - Tourist Centres	2
Welcome to Kerala	3
Kerala - Political	4
Kerala - Tourism	5
Alappuzha District	6 - 7
Ernakulam District	8 - 9
Idukki District	10 - 11
Kannur District	12 - 13
Kasargod District	14 - 15
Kollam District	16 - 17
Kottayam District	18 - 19
Kozhikode District	20 - 21

TITLE	PAGE
Malappuram District	22 - 23
Palakkad District	24 - 25
Pathanamthitta District	26 - 27
Thiruvananthapuram Distt.	28 - 29
Thrissur District	30 - 31
Wayanad District	32 - 33
Thiruvananthapuram City	34
Thiruvananthapuram - M.G. Rd. Area	35
Kochi City	36
Ernakulam City	37
Alappuzha City	38

TITLE	PAGE
Kovalam	39
Kozhikode City	40
Kottayam City & Palakkad City	41
Periyar National Park	42
Munnar City & Thrissur City	43
Varkala City & Kollam City	44
Lakshadweep	45
Major Routes from Thiruvananthapuram	46
Kerala - Distance Guide	47
Kerala - Fairs, Festivals & Index	48

Designed, Cartographed, Printed & Published by :

INDIAN MAP SERVICE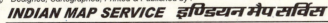

Sector 'G', Shastri Nagar, Jodhpur - 342 003 (Raj.) INDIA Tel. : (0291) 2612874
Web : www.indianmapservice.co.in, E-mail : indianmapservice@yahoo.co.in

KERALA - Political

Welcome to... ALAPPUZHA DISTRICT

Boat Race, Alappuzha

Beautiful Backwaters

Alappuzha, the water locked district is endowed with immense natural beauty and has emerged as one of the major tourist destination of the country. The sandy strip of land with Arabian Sea to its west is woven by lagoons and an array of rivers, canals, and lakes ideal for boat cruise. The main rivers are Achankovil, Pamba and Manimala. The Vembanad lake covering an area of 204 sq. kms. stretches from Alappuzha to Kochi and the Kayamkulam lake covers an area of 59.57 sq. kms. and extends into Alappuzha and Kollam districts. These lakes are used for the inland water transport of cargo and passengers.

This backwater country has been an important trading and commercial centre since time immemorial. Today, Alappuzha is well known for boat races, beaches, marine products and coir and carpet industry.

GENERAL INFORMATION

Area	: 1.417 sq. kms.
Population	: 2,109,160
Headqtrs.	: Alappuzha
Taluks	: 6
Blocks	: 12
Towns	: 11
Villages	: 91
Best Season	: Aug. -Mar.

PLACES OF INTEREST

ALAPPUZHA : The 'Venice of the East' famous for amazing backwaters, Boat Race, Houseboats, Beaches, Mullakkal Rajarajeswari Temple, Marine products and Coir industry.

Nehru Trophy Boat Race - It is held annually on the second Saturday of August at the Vembanad lake and is the most important tourist event of Alappuzha. Boats sponsored by different villages compete fiercely in the competition. The highlight of this prestigious event is "Chundan Vallam", the 130 feet long snake boats, with over 100 rowers, 4 helmsmen and 25 cheer leaders, decorated with colourful silk umbrellas. The race is also held during the tourist season on the third day of the Great Elephant March in mid January and is called as 'Tourism Snakeboat Race'.

Alappuzha - Kollam Backwater Trip - It is organised by ATDC. The journey begins at 10.30 am., and reaches Kollam at 6.00 pm. The boat passes through exotic locations and gives a close view of the scenic countryside.

AMBALAPUZHA : Pilgrim centre, Sri Krishna Temple famous for its architecture and 'Palpayasam' - a sweet milk porridge.

ARTHUNKAL PALLI : Christian pilgrim centre, St. Andrews Church here was built by Portuguese missionaries.

CHAMBAKULAM CHURCH : The St. Mary's Church, one of the oldest church in Kerala is said to be built by St. Thomas.

CHAVARA BHAVAN : The ancestral home of the blessed Kuriakose Elias Chavara. Thousands of devotees gather at this shrine and spiritual resort.

MAVELIKKARA : Chettikulangara Bhagavathy Temple famous for Kettukazhcha festival held in Feb./Mar.

EDATHUA CHURCH: It is said that prayers and offerings here help in healing mental disorders and other ailments.

KARUMADI : Famous for 9th or 10th century black granite idol of Lord Buddha known as Karumadi Kuttan.

KRISHNAPURAM PALACE : The magnificent palace is a master piece of Kerala architecture. A museum here displays antique sculptures and paintings.

KUTTANAD REGION : Land of lush paddy fields is perhaps the only region in the world where farming is done below sea level.

MANNARASHALA : Ancient temple dedicated to Sree Nagaraja, the King of Serpents.

Q S T & R BLOCK KAYAL : These regions are famous for farming over reclaimed land from the backwaters.

PATHIRAMANAL : First island resort of the State. Located in Vembanad lake and atracts rare migratory birds from various parts of the world.

ACCESSIBILITY

By Air : The nearest airport for Alappuzha is at Kochi (Nedumbassery).
By Rail : Connected by rail with Kochi, Chennai and other major cities.
By Road : The district has excellent road connections.

IMPORTANT DISTANCES FROM ALAPPUZHA

Ambalapuzha	14	Kochi	56	Palakkad	185
Arthunkal	22	Kollam	89	Painavu	141
Changanassery	25	Kottayam	43	Sabarimala	75
Edathua Church	24	Kozhikode	244	Shoranur	162
Guruvayur	136	Krishnapuram Palace	47	Sultan's Bathery	342
Kannur	334	Malappuram	206	Thalassery	308
Kasargod	400	Mannarashala	32	Thiruvananthapuram	160
Kalpetta	307	Munnar	199	Thrissur	130

ALAPPUZHA DISTRICT

Welcome to... ERNAKULAM DISTRICT

Chinese Fishing Nets

Bolghatty Palace

St. Francis Church

Synagogue, Mattancherry

Ernakulam district is the first fully literate district in the country and is also the most industrially developed district of the State. Kochi, the district heaquarter is recognised as the 'Commercial Capital' and the most cosmopolitan city of Kerala. There are many prestigious large and medium scale industries in the industrial belt covering Ernakulam - Kalamassery-Eloor and Aluva. Besides this there are large number of small scale and cottage industries. The district is known for production of timber, copra, coir, rubber and rice etc. It is also endowed with rich mineral deposits.

The district is also a tourist's haven and is famous for its Chinese fishing nets, Portuguese architecture, churches, Jewish synagogues, scenic beauty and handicrafts.

GENERAL INFORMATION

Area	: 3,068 sq. kms.
Population	: 3,105,798
Headqtrs.	: Ernakulam
Taluks	: 7
Blocks	: 15
Towns	: 28
Villages	: 117
Best Season	: Sept. - May.

PLACES OF INTEREST

ALUVA (ALWAYE): Pilgrim centre and summer resort. The Periyar river here is considered ideal for bathing.
ANGAMALI: Fastest growing town in Kerala. The Little Flower Hospital here is perhaps the largest eye hospital in South India.
BHUTHATHANKETTU: Picnic spot, Trekking.
CHENNAMANGALAM: Jewish centre, Synagogue, Nearby ruins of the Vypeenkotta seminary built by the Portuguese.
CHOWARRA: Summer resort of Cochin royal family. Centre for mat weaving and rattan work.
EDAPPALLY: Famous for Museum of Kerala History and its Makers, M. N. F Gallery of Paintings & Sculptures.
KALADI: Hindu pilgrim centre. Birth place of Adi Sankaracharya, the great Advaitha philosopher and Bhakti saint of 8th century.
KALLIL: Historians and archaeological centre. Famous for the rock cut caves housing Jain monuments.
KOCHI - ERNAKULAM: Kochi, the "Queen of the Arabian Sea" has one of the finest natural harbours in the world and is one of the oldest port in country. Ernakulam, the "Gateway to Kochi' is the commercial and residential part of the twin city. The main attractions are - Chinese Fishing Nets, Beach, Santa Cruz Basilica, St. Francis Church, Vasco House, VOC Gate, Bishop's House, Fort Immanuel, Dutch Cemetery, Willingdon Island, Vypin Island, Bolghatty Palace at Bolghatty Island etc.
Mattancherry - Commercial hub of Kochi, Jewish Synagogue and Jew Town, Koonan Kurishu Chapel and Dutch Palace.
KODANAD: Elephant training centre, Mini zoo.
KOTHAMANGALAM: 14th century St. Thomas Church of the Orthodox Syrians and the St. Mary's Church are main attractions.
MALAYATTUR: Christian pilgrim centre famous for the St. Thomas Church, one of the greatest Catholic churches in the State. Annual feast falls in the month of Mar. / Apr.
PIRAVAM: St. Mary's Church, one of the oldest church of Kerala, Sculptures and paintings.
THATTEKAD BIRD SANC.: First bird sanctuary of Kerala. Water birds and other rare species of birds can be seen here. Best season - Sept. - Mar.
TRIPUNITTURA: Seat of erstwhile Cochin Rajas. Main attractions - Sri Poornathreyesa Temple and Hill Palace Museum exhibiting the riches and fortunes of the Cochin Rajas. Tripunittura is also known for 'Athachamayam' - a spectacular procession which marks the beginning of Onam festival and the world famous 'Sahyadri International Ayurvedic Centre'.

ACCESSIBILITY

By Air: The domestic airport is at Kochi and international is at Nedumbassery.
By Rail: Ernakulam - Kochi are well connected by trains.
By Road: Well developed road network.
ByFerry: Ferry connections.

IMPORTANT DISTANCES FROM KOCHI

Alappuzha	56	Kalpetta	251	Palakkad	135
Aluva (Alwaye)	25	Kozhikode	188	Painavu	99
Angamali	40	Kottayam	66	Sabarimala	134
Changanassery	84	Kollam	145	Shoranur	106
Guruvayur	80	Kothamangalam	55	Sultan's Bathery	286
Kannur	278	Malappuram	150	Thalassery	255
Kasargod	344	Malayattur	53	Thiruvananthapuram	220
Kaladi	45	Munnar	153	Thrissur	79

ERNAKULAM DISTRICT

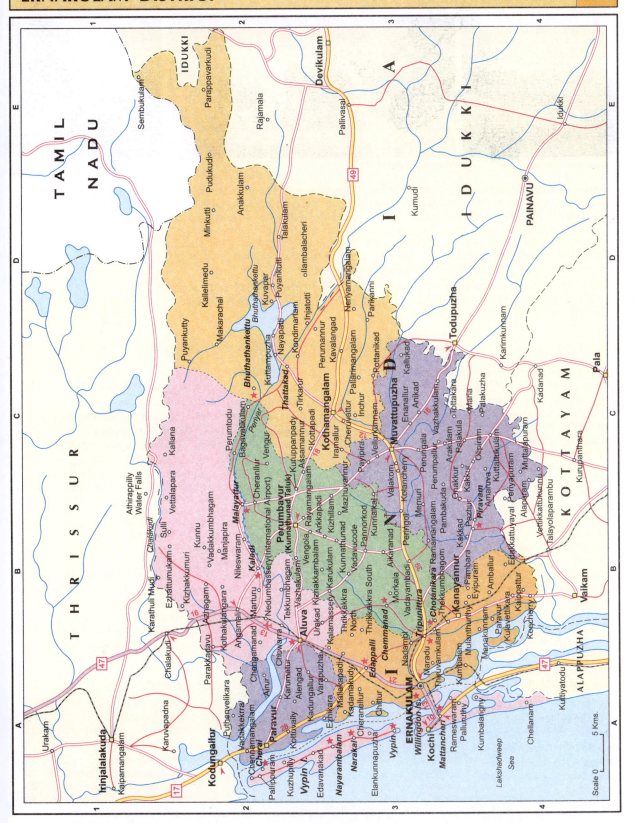

Welcome to... IDUKKI DISTRICT

Scenic View, Munnar

Elephants at Periyar WLS

River View, Idukki

Idukki, the hilly district of Kerala gets the name from Malayalam word 'Idukku', which means a narrow gorge. The charming district is the most nature rich areas of Kerala and teems with picturesque peaks and verdant valleys. Its 1500 sq. kms. reserved forest area is a haven for enchanting wildlife and exotic flora. The district is watered by three main rivers - Periyar, Thalayar and Thodupuzhayar and is referred as the "Power-House" of the Kerala, as about 60% of the States power needs are fulfilled by the hydro-electric power station at Moolamattom. Idukki s also well known for its tea industry and pepper.

Wildlife sanctuaries, hill stations, spice plantation tours, trekking and elephant rides are some of the attractions of this beautiful district. It is also home to large number of tribal population known for their unique customs and beliefs.

GENERAL INFORMATION

Area	: 4,476 sq. kms.
Population	: 1,129,221
Headqtrs.	: Painavu
Taluks	: 4
Blocks	: 8
Towns	: 2
Villages	: 65
Best Season	: Aug. - Mar.

PLACES OF INTEREST

CHERUTHONI : Breathtaking scenic beauty.

CHINNAR WILDLIFE SANC. : Rich wildlife, Trekking.

ERAVIKULAM - RAJAMALAI WILDLIFE SANCTUARY: Largest population of Nilgiri Tahr. Other animals - sambar, giant Malabar squirrel, tiger, panther, nilgiri langur. Best season - Nov. to April.

IDUKKI ARCH DAM : World's second and Asia's first arch dam. The **Idukki Wildlife Sanctuary** is located nearby which is comparable to the famous Periyar National Park. Key fauna - sambar and elephant. Best Season - Nov. to May.

KEEZHARKUTH : Waterfalls, Forests of medicinal plants, Mountaineering and trekking.

MALANKARA : Famous picnic spot. The artificial lake here was built as a part of Muvattupuzha Valley Irrigation Project.

MARAYOOR : Sandalwood forests, Sandalwood factory, Rock cut caves with murals.

MATTUPETTY: Indo - Swiss dairy project, exotic cattle, rose garden and lush green meadows.

Nearby attractions - **Top Station** and **Kundale**.

MUNNAR : Beautiful hill resort dotted with lakes, reservoirs, forests and tea estates and plantations. Munnar also has the highest peak in South India, **Anai Mudi**, which rises over 2695 m. and is an ideal spot for trekking.

Around Munnar

Attukal (9 kms.) : Scenic beauty and waterfalls.

Chithirapuram (10 kms.) : Hill station, Tea plantations.

Devikulam (7 kms.) : Hill resort, Lake and Tea plantations.

Nyayamakad (10 kms.) : Waterfalls, Picnic spot.

Pallivasal (8 kms.) : First hydro electric project in Kerala.

Pothamedu (6 kms.) : Scenic beauty, Plantations.

PERIYAR WILDLIFE SANC., THEKKADI : One of the most popular wildlife sanctuary of the country and southern most tiger reserve of India. Key fauna - Tiger, elephants, bison, sambar, spotted deer, leopard, Malabar flying squirrel, Nilgiri langurs, Nilgiri tahr, rich variety of migratory and resident birds etc. Park is also known for its rich floral wealth, scenic beauty and bracing climate.

PIRMED : Summer resort of erstwhile Travancore Rajas, Plantation town, Waterfalls, Trekking.

Peeru Hills (4 kms.) : Paradise for trekkers and picnickers. Mausoleum of Peer Mohammed, Summer palace of the erstwhile royal family and the residence of the Diwan.

SURYANELLY : Hill resort, Lake and Tea plantations.

WAGAMON : Hill resort, Tea gardens and Meadows. It will be one of the leading eco-tourism projects of India.

ACCESSIBILITY

By Air : Kochi is the nearest airport from Idukki.

By Rail : Nearest railheads are at Kochi and Kottayam.

By Road : Important towns of the district are well connected by road.

IMPORTANT DISTANCES FROM MUNNAR

Alappuzha	199	Kollam	261	Sabarimala	189
Changanassery	174	Kottayam	156	Shoranur	192
Chinnar WLS	70	Kozhikode	287	Sultan's Bathery	338
Guruvayur	179	Malappuram	232	Suryanelly	27
Kannur	377	Marayoor	36	Thalassery	354
Kasargod	443	Mattupetty	13	Thekkady (Periyar N.P.)	106
Kalpetta	350	Painavu	60	Thiruvananthapuram	304
Kochi	153	Palakkad	221	Thrissur	160

Welcome to... KANNUR DISTRICT

Kalaripayattu

Fort St. Angelo, Kannur

Payyambalam Beach, Kannur

Kannur district is flanked by the Western Ghats in the east and Lakshadweep sea in the west. It has a long coastline interspersed with many rivers, coconut - fringed lagoons and beautiful backwaters. The district is rich in natural resources and has a flourishing traditional handloom industry. It is also the centre for production of cashew nut, copra, rice, tiles, electric bulb, hard board and plywood.

The district has contributed immensely to the cultural, religious, political and industrial heritage of the State. It is an important centre of various colourful folk arts and folk music of

GENERAL INFORMATION

Area	: 2,966 sq. kms.
Population	: 2,412,365
Headqtrs.	: Kanuur
Taluks	: 3
Blocks	: 9
Towns	: 45
Villages	: 127
Best Season	: Aug. - Mar.

PLACES OF INTEREST

ANJARAKANDI : Cinnamon plantations here are said to be the biggest in Asia.

ARALAM WILDLIFE SANCTUARY : Key fauna - elephant, sloth bear, mouse deer etc. Rich variety of birds and reptiles can also be seen.

EZHIMALA : Picturesque hilly town besides the sea, Beautiful beach, Ancient mosque.

KANNUR : Historical town, Formerly a major port referred as "a great emporia of spice trade" in Marco Polo's travel records. Also famous for handloom industry and cashew nut trading.

St. Angelo's Fort : Triangular fort overlooking the Arabian Sea was built in 1505, by the Portuguese.

Payyambalam Beach : Long, clean and quiet beach.

MADAYI : Well known for the 12th century mosque built by Malik Iban Dinar and fine beach.

MAHE : Scenic enclave of Pondicherry UT, famous for the sea skirting roads and unique culture with French flavour.

PARASSINIKADAVU : Famous for a unique snake farm dedicated to the preservation and conservation of snakes.

Other important attraction is the **Parassinikadavu Muthappan Temple** known for its ritual art form "Muthappan Theyyam".

PAZHASSI DAM : Picnic site and boating.

PAITHAL MALA : Small hill resort rich in flora and fauna.

TALIPARAMBA : Famous for Raja Rajeswara Temple and Trichambaram Temple.

THALASSERY : Historical town famous for producing most of the India's circus artists.

Thalassery Fort - Magnificent fort on the Thalassery beach was built by the British in 1708. The grand gateway and a lighthouse are major attractions.

Arrackal Kottaram - Residence of Arrackal Ali Rajas, the only Muslim royal family in the State.

Gundert Bungalow - Residence of German scholar Rev. Dr. Herman Gundert, who compiled the first Malayalam dictionary and published the first newspaper in Malayalam. He also built a church on Nettur Hill in 1889.

Muzhappilangad Beach - Located on the Thalassery - Kannur route, it is one of the longest and cleanest beaches in the State.

THIRUVANGAD : Famous for Sree Ramaswami Temple adorned with exquisite carvings.

ACCESSIBILITY

By Air : The nearest airport Karipur, Kozhikode.

By Rail : Kannur is one of the important railway station of Southern India.

By Road : The district has good road network.

IMPORTANT DISTANCES FROM KANNUR

Alappuzha	334	Kottayam	344	Pazhassi Dam	37
Aralam WLS	35	Kozhikode	90	Sabarimala	412
Changannassery	362	Madayi	22	Shoranur	183
Ezhimala	55	Malappuram	125	Sultan's Bathery	150
Guruvayur	198	Munnar	377	Thalassery	20
Kasargod	66	Painavu	377	Thiruvangad	23
Kalpetta	115	Paithal Mala	65	Thiruvananthapuram	465
Kochi	278	Palakkad	209	Thrissur	223
Kollam	423	Parassinikadavu	16		

KANNUR DISTRICT

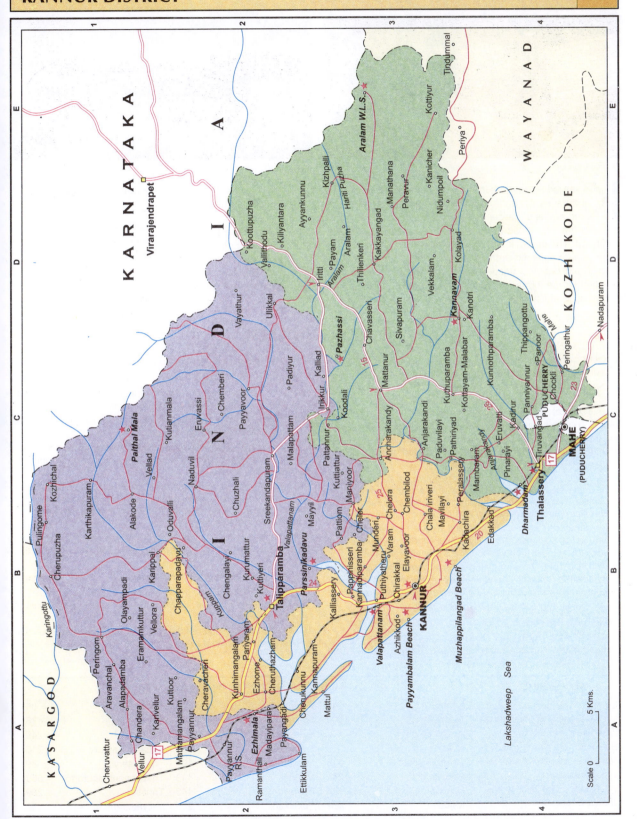

Welcome to... KASARGOD DISTRICT

Theyyam Dancer

Bekal Fort

Kasargod is the northernmost district of Kerala and is famous for its coir and handloom industries. It is endowed with rich natural resources. The coastal region is full of coconut and arecanut gardens while the midlands have extensive paddy fields. The important crops in the hilly areas include rubber, cashew and ginger. Fishing is the prime source of livelihood. The district is also known as a land of fabulous fantasies, as it abounds in sacred temples with splendid architecture, majestic forts, ravishing rivers, undulating hills, verdant valleys and beautiful unspoilt beaches. The rich culture of the district is displayed through spectacular performances of Theyyam, Yakshagana, Kumbla (buffalo race), Poorakkali, Kolkali etc., which linger for a long time in the memories of the visitors.

GENERAL INFORMATION

Area	: 1,961 sq. kms.
Population	: 1,203,342
Headqtrs.	: Kasargod
Taluks	: 2
Blocks	: NA
Towns	: 6
Villages	: 116
Best Season	: Aug. - Mar.

PLACES OF INTEREST

ADOOR: Ancient temple of Sree Mahalingeswara dedicated to Siva on the banks of river Payaswani amidst lush woods.

AJANUR: Madiyam Kovilakam Temple, an ancient shrine of goddess Bhadrakali famous for intricate wood carvings and various cultural and religious programmes.

ANANTHAPURA: 9th century temple set in a rock cut lake is the only lake temple in Kerala. It is said to be the 'moolasthanam' or the original seat of Anathapadmanabha of Sree Padmanabha Swami Temple in Thiruvananthapuram.

BEKAL: The mighty fort here was built by Shivappa Naik in 1650. It came under Tipu Sultan in 18th century and was later occupied by the British. The observation towers of the fort afford breath taking views of the scenic surroundings and the beautiful beach.

Other attractions are Pallikere Beach, Bekal Hole Aqua Park, Kappil Beach (6 kms.), Kodi Cliffs and famous spiritual centre Anandasram (15 km.) founded in 1939, by Swami Ramdas.

CHANDRAGIRI: 17th century fort affording breathtaking views of Lakshadweep Sea and Chandragiri river. Excellent sun-set point, Mosque and ancient Kizhur Sastha Temple located nearby.

BELA: 'Our Lady of Sorrow' church built in 1890.

CHERUVATHUR: Relics of 18th century Dutch fort, Picnic spot.

KANHANGAD/ HOSDURG FORT: Chain of forts built by Somashekara Nayak, Karpooreswara Temple and World renowned spiritual centre - Nithyanandashram.

KASARGOD: Fort built by Sivappa Nayak in 17th century.

KOTTANCHERRY: Scenic beauty, Trekking.

KUMBLA: Scenic lagoon, Parthasarathi temple at Mujankavu, Gopalakrishna temple & Ananthapura temple.

MADHUR: Pilgrim centre famous for Srimad Anantheswara Vinayaka or Mahaganapathi Temple.

MANJESHWARA: Srimad Ananteswar or Mahalingeshwar temple and many shrines, Fifteen mosques, Birth place of M. Govind Pai, Cashew growing town.

NILESHWARAM: Cultural centre of the Kasargod district. There are several 'Kavus', where nature, God and man commune in serene silence. The Nileshwaram Palace is now the folklore centre of the Dept. of Archaeology.

PANDIYAN KALLU: A rock rises in the sea about 2 kms. from Trikkannad temple. It is considered ideal for adventurous swimming.

RANIPURAM: Lush forests and grasslands, Trekking, Elephants and other wildlife.

THALANKARA: Famous for Malik Deener Juma Masjid built in typical Kerala style.

VALIYAPARAMBA: One of the most scenic backwater stretch in Kerala. Enchanting boat cruise.

ACCESSIBILITY

By Air: The nearest airport for Kasargod is at Mangalore (50 kms.) in Karnataka.

By Rail: Kasargod is connected by rail with several important towns.

By Road: The district has good road network.

IMPORTANT DISTANCES FROM KASARGOD

Adoor	45	Kochi	344	Ranipuram	85
Alappuzha	400	Kollam	489	Sabarimala	478
Ananthapura	12	Kottayam	410	Shoranur	249
Bekal	16	Kozhikode	156	Sultan's Bathery	216
Changanassery	428	Malappuram	191	Thalassery	89
Guruvayur	264	Munnar	443	Thiruvananthapuram	560
Kannur	66	Painavu	443	Thrissur	289
Kalpetta	181	Palakkad	275	Valiyaparamba	30

KASARGOD DISTRICT 15

Welcome to... KOLLAM DISTRICT

A House Boat

Govt. Guest House, Kollam

Kollam district is a veritable Kerala in miniature, reflecting all the colours of Kerala kaleidoscope. The district has immense tourist potential as it is blessed by nature's bounty. It has beautiful beaches and backwaters, meandering rivers, lovely lakes, majestic mountains, verdant valleys, lush forests, fertile plains with vast green fields producing tropical crops. It also has historic monuments and numerous temples built in the traditional architectural style.

The district has about 37.3 kms. long coastline and has a good network of backwaters and canals. It also has fairly developed coir and bamboo industry. The handicrafts produce include screw-pine fancy goods, cane and rattan works, paddy straw pictures and wood carving.

GENERAL INFORMATION

Area	: 2,491 sq. kms.
Population	: 2,584,118
Headqtrs.	: Kollam
Taluks	: 5
Blocks	: NA
Towns	: 7
Villages	: 92
Best Season	: Aug. - Mar.

PLACES OF INTEREST

ARIYANKAVU : Sastha temple famous for Mandalapooja and Thrikkalyanam festivals in December. The 2.5 kms. long tunnel on Konkan Railway. **Palaruvi Waterfalls** (5 kms.) are worth visiting.

JATAYUPARA, CHATAYAMANGALAM : A huge rock here is named after the mythical bird Jatayu from the epic Ramayana.

KOLLAM : Major centre of cashew trading and processing. One of the oldest and flourishing sea port on the Arabian Sea.

Ashtamudi Lake - Scenic lake amidst red cliffs and swaying palms. Extensive facilities for retting coconut husks, which makes the district hub of coir industry. The Chinese fishing nets add to the spectacular scenic beauty of the lake.

Backwater Tours - Kollam is also renowned as the 'Gateway to Kerala's Beautiful Backwater'. The eight hour backwater cruise between Kollam and Alappuzha is the best and most comprehensive introduction to the magical backwaters of Kerala.

House Boats - For soothing, calming and nourishing experience of Kerala's house boat contact the DTPC tourist information centre near the boat jetty.

Kochupilamodu Beach - Excellent model park at the beach.

Crafts Festival - Held annually in Dec. - Jan.

Thangasseri (5 kms.) - Historical seaside village, ruins of Portuguese fort, colonial buildings, churches and light house.

Thirumullavaram Beach (6 kms.) - Popular picnic spot.

KOLATHUPUZHA : Famous for Sastha temple and Vishu Mahotsavam held in Apr. / May.

MAYYANAD : Subramanya temple at Umayanallor and several other important shrines.

OCHIRA : Unique Parabrahma Temple dedicated to 'Universal Consciousness'. Ochira Kali in mid. June and Panthrandu Vilakku in Nov. / Dec. are the two main annual festivals. Important handicraft centre.

PICNIC VILLAGE, ASHRAMAM : Important recreational centre located along the backwaters. The tourist complex has a 200 year old Govt. Guest House, Adventure Park, Boat Club, Children's Traffic Park and Yatri Niwas.

PUNALUR : Industrial centre, Suspension bridge built in 1879, over Kallada river is a star attraction. The Lord Ayyappa temple at Sasthamkonam is very popular.

SASTHAMKOTTA : Temple of Lord Sastha, Sasthamkotta Lake - the only major fresh water lake in the State.

SHENDURUNY WILDLIFE SANC. : Key fauna - Elephant, Tiger, Leopard, Bear etc. Rich floral wealth.

THENMALA : Dam site, Tea and Rubber plantations.

VALLIKAVU : Headquarters of Matha Amrithanandamayi Devi Ashram at Amrithapuri.

ACCESSIBILITY

By Air : Nearest airport is at Thiruvananthapuram.

By Rail : Kollam is an important railhead.

By Road : Well developed road network.

By Ferry : Ferry station near central bus station.

IMPORTANT DISTANCES FROM KOLLAM

Alappuzha	89	Kolathupuzha	64	Sabarimala	93
Ariyankavu	70	Kottayam	105	Sasthamkotta	29
Changanassery	69	Kozhikode	333	Shoranur	251
Guruvayur	225	Malappuram	295	Sultan's Bathery	431
Kannur	423	Munnar	261	Thalassery	400
Kasargod	489	Ochira	34	Thenmala	66
Kalpetta	396	Painavu	172	Thiruvananthapuram	71
Kochi	145	Palakkad	280	Thrissur	219

KOLLAM DISTRICT

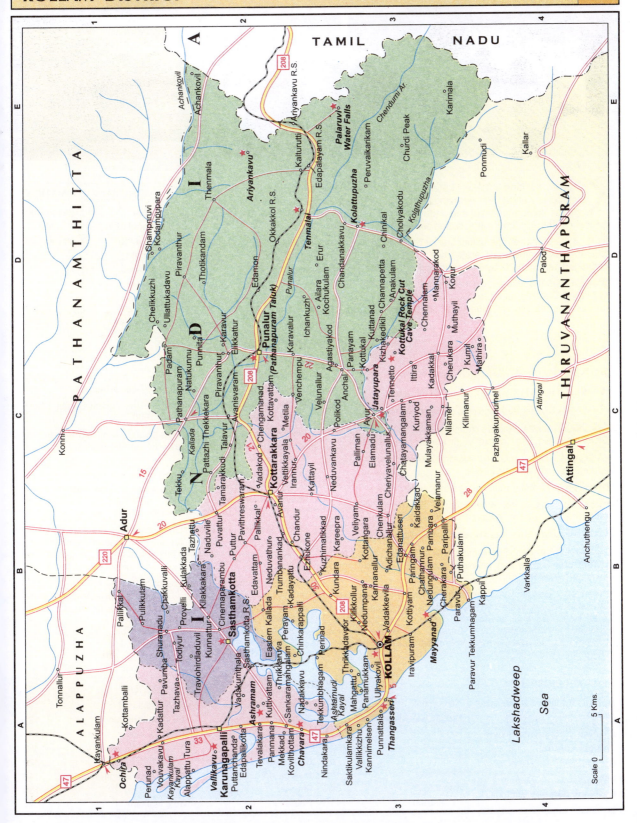

Welcome to... KOTTAYAM DISTRICT

Beautiful Backwaters

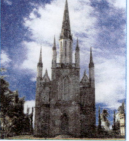
Syrian Church

Soothing Coconut trees

Kottayam, the land of 'Lakes, Latex and Letters' is one of the most industrially developed districts of Kerala. This amazing land is flanked by the lofty Western Ghats on the east and the Vembanad Lake and paddy fields of Kuttanad in the west. The district is a large producer of rubber, coconut, tea, coffee and pepper.

This land of letters has the distinction of being the highest literate district in the country and Kottayam was the first total literate town in the country. The first Malayalam printing press was established here in 1820, by Benjamin Bailey, a Christian missionary.

Kottayam district is also known for its religious harmony and has numerous temples, churches and a 1000 year old mosque. Kottayam town is an ideal base for visiting various important tourist centres like Pirmed, Munnar, Idukki, Ernakulam etc.

GENERAL INFORMATION

Area	: 2,208 sq. kms.
Population	: 1,952,901
Headqtrs.	: Kottayam
Taluks	: 5
Blocks	: 11
Towns	: 8
Villages	: 95
Best Season	: Sept. - Mar.

PLACES OF INTEREST

ADIRUMPUZHA: St. Mary's Church built in 1080 AD.

ARUVIKKUZHI WATERFALLS : Beautiful picnic site.

AYYAMPARA : Scenic surroundings, excellent sunset viewing.

BHARANANGANAM : Ancient church housing the mortal remains of Sister Alphonsa. The Grotto of Virgin Mary is very attractive.

CHANGANASSERY : Acient Thrikkodithanam temple famous for 'Deepam' festival held in Nov. - Dec.

Pazhayapalli - Famous 1000 years old mosque.

Peruna- Well known for Kidangoor Sri Subrhamanya Swamy Temple and Sree Sankara Ayurveda Vaidyasala.

ERUMELI : Pilgrim centre, Lord Sastha temple, Ancient Mosque.

ETTUMANUR : Ancient Siva temple built in 16 A.D., noted for its excellent architecture and splendid sculptures. 10 day temple festival celebrated in Feb. / Mar.

KOTTAYAM : Beautiful backwater town and important trading centre also known as the 'Mecca of Publishing Industry' in the Kerala state. Several newspapers (dailies), magazines and periodicals in Malayalam and English are published here. Stronghold of Christians and has numerous ancient churches.

St. Mary's Church, Cheriyapally - It has exquisite murals and paintings depicting Biblical and non - Biblical themes.

St. Mary's Church, Valiyapalli - The ancient Syrian Christian church is said to have been built in 1550.

Thirunakkara Siva Temple - It is a good example of Kerala style of architecture. 'Phalguna Utsav', the annual festival is celebrated during March.

KUMARAKOM : Famous for bird sanctuary, backwaters and boat cruise. Birds seen at the sanctuary on the eastern bank of Vembanad Lake are - water fowl, cuckoo, owl, ducks and migratory birds like Siberian storks. Best Season - Jun. - Aug.

MANNANAM : This Syrian Christian pilgrim centre is 8 kms. from Kottayam and is famous for the St. Joseph's monastery. St. Joseph's Press established in 1844, is one of the oldest printing press in Kerala.

VAIKAM : Famous for the legendary Siva Temple believed to be built by Lord Parasuram. The 12 day *Ashtami* festival held in Nov. / Dec. is known for its elephant processions, religious discourses and traditional dances and music.

ACCESSIBILITY

By Air : Kochi is the nearest airport from Kottayam.

By Rail : Kottayam is well connected by rail.

By Road : Excellent road network.

By Ferry : Two ferry stations.

IMPORTANT DISTANCES FROM KOTTAYAM

Alappuzha	43	Kalpetta	211	Palakkad	196
Aruvikkuzhi Waterfalls	18	Kochi	66	Sabarimala	121
Ayyampara	43	Kollam	105	Shoranur	167
Changanassery	18	Kozhikode	254	Sultan's Bathery	352
Erumeli	60	Kumarakom	16	Thalassery	321
Guruvayur	146	Malappuram	210	Thiruvananthapuram	148
Kannur	344	Munnar	156	Thrissur	135
Kasaragod	410	Painavu	116	Vaikam	40

KOTTAYAM DISTRICT

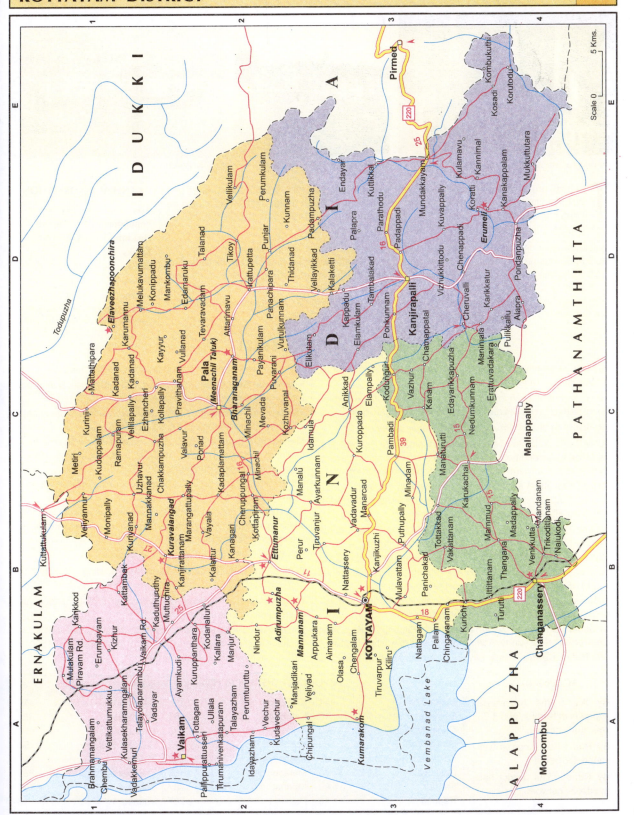

Welcome to... KOZHIKODE DISTRICT

Site where Vasco da Gama first landed, Kappad

Mananchira Square, Kozhikode

Kappad Beach

The lush green district teems with serene beaches, verdant hills, wildlife sanctuaries and historic sites. The district occupies an important position in Indian history, as Vasco da Gama landed at Kappad (16 kms. north of Kozhikode) in 1498, and discovered the sea route to India. This marked the advent of European powers in India.

Kozhikode is an industrially developed district. It is well known for the timber industry. The traditional industries of the district are handloom, coir, cashew, bricks, tiles and handicrafts. The tiles from Kozhikode district are famous all over the country and are also exported. Agriculture is the mainstay of districts economy. The main crops grown are coffee, tea, rubber, pepper, coconut, arecanut, tapioca, sugar cane etc. An agricultural research station at Koothali and the coconut nursery at Thikkodi are the important institutions of their kind.

GENERAL INFORMATION

Area	: 2,345 sq. kms.
Population	: 2,878,498
Headqtrs.	: Kozhikode
Taluks	: 3
Blocks	: 12
Towns	: 18
Villages	: 117
Best Season	: Sept. - May.

PLACES OF INTEREST

BEYPORE : Port town and ancient trading centre. Famous for its ship building yard and traditional ship builders.

CHELIYA : Kathakali Vidhyalayam, a training centre for Kathakali dance. Kathakali classes and special performances are held.

FEROKH : Famous for tiles, pottery and ceramic wares.

KAPPAD : On 27th May 1498, Vasco da Gama from Portugal first landed here. A monument here commemorates the historic event. There is also an ancient temple on a hillock overlooking the sea.

KADALUNDI BIRD SANC. : A paradise for bird watchers. Large number of migratory birds like terns, gulls, herons, sandpipers, whimbrels, etc., visit these islands from Nov. - Apr.

KAKKAYAM : Picturesque dam site. The scenic landscape teems with wildlife and is also ideal for trekking and rock climbing.

KOZHIKODE (CALICUT) : Capital of Zamorins. It attained a position of pre-eminence in the trade of pepper and other spices and still retains the glory and charm of the bygone era.

Pazhassi Raja Museum - It displays ancient mural paintings, antique bronzes, old coins, models of temples etc.

Art Gallery & Krishna Menon Museum - Paintings of Raja Ravi Varma & Raja Raja Varma. A section dedicated to Krishna Menon.

CVN Kalari Centre - Kalaripayattu, the martial art of Kerala is performed here. Special demonstrations are held here.

Kozhikode Beach - Beautiful beach, Old light house, Sunset point, Lions Park and the Marine Water Aquarium.

Tali Temple - 14th century shrine built by Swamy Thirumulpad, the Zamorin. A fine example of Kerala architecture.

Mananchira Square - The historic *maidan* is now an arcadia with beautiful trees and plants, artificial hills, sculptures, open air theatre and musical fountain.

Other places of interest in Kozhikode town are the Planetarium and Regional Science Centre.

KUTTICHIRA : The Muccunti Mosque here has a stone inscription, which reveals the history of powerful Zamorins. The Mishkal Masjid is another important mosque.

PAYYOLI : Famous for an old fort and mosque.

PERUVANNAMUZHI DAM : Dam site, Boating, Crocodile farm and Bird sanctuary.

TUSHARAGIRI : Famous for evergreen forests, exotic birds, wildlife and exciting trekking trails.

VADAKARA : Ancient town has relics of a fort, associated with Tacholi Othenan, the hero of ballads of North Malabar. 1500 year old Lokanarkavu Bhagavathi Temple.

ACCESSIBILITY

By Air : The Kozhikode airport is at Karipur, about 23 kms. from the town.

By Rail : Kozhikode is well connected by rail.

By Road : The district has good road network.

IMPORTANT DISTANCES FROM KOZHIKODE

Alappuzha	244	Kasargod	156	Palakkad	119
Beypore	10	Kalpetta	63	Sabarimala	322
Changanassery	272	Kochi	188	Shoranur	93
Guruvayur	108	Kollam	333	Sultan's Bathery	98
Kadalundi Bird Sanc.	25	Kottayam	254	Thalassery	67
Kakkayam	45	Malappuram	50	Thiruvananthapuram	382
Kannur	90	Munnar	287	Thrissur	134
Kappad	16	Painavu	287	Vadakara	48

KOZHIKODE DISTRICT

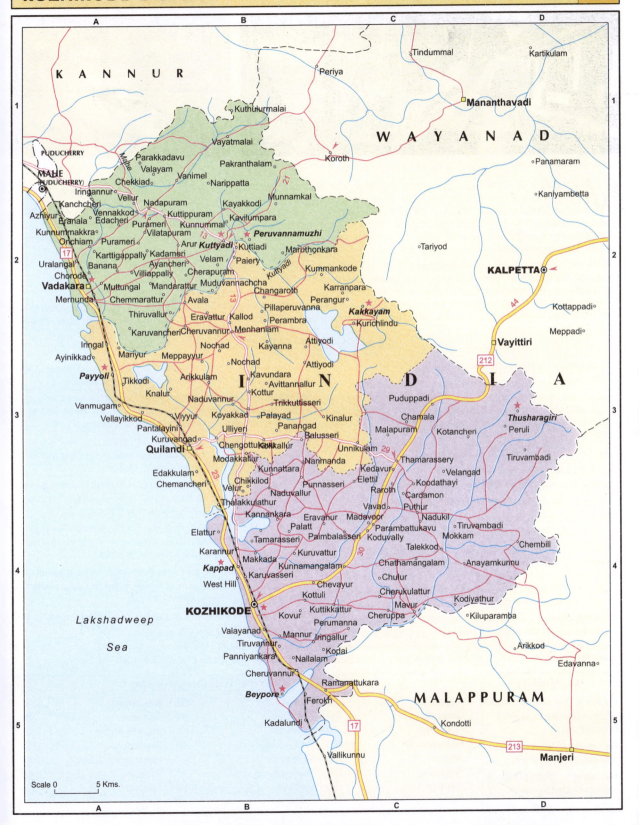

Welcome to... MALAPPURAM DISTRICT

Kerala Aruvedic Treatment

Malappuram or a 'terraced place atop the hills', comprises of undulating hills with innumerable streams flowing through them and reaching the coconut fringed sea coast. These streams at places are linked with the backwaters, facilitating network of inland waterways. The hilly tracts have dense forests and extensive teak plantations. The main crops produced here are paddy, coconut, arecanut, cashewnut, pepper, ginger, pulses, banana, tapioca and rubber.

The district has also immensely contributed to the rich cultural traditions of Kerala and has been a centre for Hindu - Vedic learning and teaching. This land of beaches, backwaters, hills and valleys is the headquarters of the traditional Indian medicinal system of Ayurveda. Ponnani, the taluk headquarters, is an important centre for education in the philosophy of Islam. The temples and mosques of the district are known for their colourful festivals.

GENERAL INFORMATION

Area	: 3,550 sq. kms.
Population	: 3,629,640
Headqtrs.	: Malappuram
Taluks	: 4
Blocks	: 14
Towns	: 5
Villages	: 123
Best Season	: Sept. - Mar.

PLACES OF INTEREST

ADYANPARA : Waterfalls and lush forests.

ANGADIPPURAM : Religious centre for Hindus and Muslims. The principal deities of the Thirumandhankunnu temple are Goddess Bhagavathi and Lord Shiva. Tali temple is the other important shrine in the town. The Puthanangadi mosque has Arabic inscriptions engraved on one of its planks.

ARIKKOD : Centre of pottery and timber trade.

KADAMPUZHA : The famous Bhagvathi temple here is said to have been consecrated by Jagatguru Sankaracharya.

KARUVARAKKUNDU : Large plantations of rubber, tea etc.

KONDOTTI : The 500 year old Pazhayangadi Mosque here is known for Valia Nercha festival held in Feb. - Mar.

KOTTAKKAL : The historical town has a fortified palace of the Kizhakke Kovilakam kings, but is now famous for the Kottakkal Arya Vaidyasala, a pioneering institute of Ayurveda. It specialises in the Kerala's traditional system of health and medicine and has an Ayurvedic research centre and a hospital.

MALAPPURAM : It was the military headquarters of the Zamorins of Kozhikode and has a rich and eventful history. The ruins of Tipu Sultan's fort can still be seen here. The Jama-at Mosque here is known for Nercha festival held in April. Adjacent to the mosque is the mausoleum of the Malappuram Shaheeds, whose brave exploits have been immortalised in the Mappilla balads.

MAMBURAM : Muslim pilgrim centre famous for the Makham, a shrine used primarily as a receptacle for the dead bodies of *Thangals*, the religious leaders of Malabar Muslims.

MANJERI : The historical town is noted for the Karikkad Subramania temple. The temple at Trikkalangode, near Manjeri is known for the Manjeri Pooram festival (April).

NILAMBUR : The Nilambur forest area is famous for the 'Canolly's Plot', said to be the world's oldest teak plantation. Home of Cholanaickans, the oldest aboriginal tribe of Kerala.

TANUR : The coastal fishing town has earliest Portuguese settlements. The Keraladeshapuram temple of Vishnu is located nearby and is one of the oldest temple of Kerala.

TIRUR : Birth place of Tunchath Ramanujan Ezhuthassan, the father of Malayalam literature. Large number of kids are initiated into the process of writing over here.

THIRUNAVAYA (8 kms.) - Thirunavaya Navamukunda temple and annual Sarvodaya Mela (fair).

VALLIKUNNU BEACH : Scenic beach resort amidst coconut groove. Kadalundi Bird Sanctuary is located nearby.

ACCESSIBILITY

By Air : The nearest airport for Malappuram is at Karipur (Kozhikode).

By Rail : Nearest main railhead is at Kozhikode.

By Road : Malappuram is well connected by road.

IMPORTANT DISTANCES FROM MALAPPURAM

Alappuzha	206	Kollam	295	Sabarimala	284
Changanassery	234	Kottakkal	12	Shoranur	48
Guruvayur	70	Kottayam	210	Sultan's Bathery	152
Kadampuzha	30	Kozhikode	50	Thalassery	102
Kannur	125	Munnar	232	Thiruvananthapuram	366
Kasargod	191	Nilambur	37	Thrissur	95
Kalpetta	98	Painavu	208	Tirur	25
Kochi	150	Palakkad	80		

MALAPPURAM DISTRICT

Welcome to... PALAKKAD DISTRICT

Malampuzha Garden

Lush Paddy Fields

The mighty Gaur

Picturesque Palakkad district, the 'Granary' or the 'Rice Bowl' of Kerala is set in the foot of majestic Western Ghats and is unique in its geographical position, historical background, educational status and tourist attractions. The district receives high rain from both south-west and north-east winds which helps in bumper paddy crop. Other important crops grown here are, sugarcane, groundnut, arecanut, cotton, rubber, cardamom, coffee and cashewnut etc.

The district has several irrigation projects and rivers. Bharathapuzha or Ponnani river, originates from Anamalai hills and is the longest river of Kerala. Handloom weaving is the important traditional industry of the district.

GENERAL INFORMATION

Area	: 4,480 sq. kms.
Population	: 2,617,072
Headqtrs.	: Palakkad
Taluks	: 5
Blocks	: 13
Towns	: 5
Villages	: 163
Best Season	: Sept. - Feb.

PLACES OF INTEREST

ALATTUR : Atop the Alattur or Velimala hill near the town are the ruins of an ancient temple and a perennial natural spring.

ATTAPPADI : The hilly region on the crest of the Western Ghats is home to the oldest tribal settlements of Kerala. It abounds in verdant valleys, forests, plantations, paddy fields and numerous streamlets.

CHITTUR : Famous for the Kongappa festival (Feb. - Mar.), Tunchat Acharyamadom and crafts like Kora grass mat making and granite carving.

DHONI : Reserve forest, Waterfall.

KOLLANGOD : Palace, Vishnu temple, Trekking.

MALAMPUZHA : Famous for scenic surroundings and beautiful picnic spots. Main attractions Malampuzha dam, Rose gardens and amusement park, boating, fishing etc.

MANGALAM DAM : Picnic site.

NELLIAMPATHI : Hill resort, Teak plantations, Orange estates, Picnic spots.

PALAKKAD : Cultural and historical centre. A granite fort here was built by Hyder Ali of Mysore in 1766 and is the best preserved fort of Kerala. Other attractions includes, Kalpathy Siva temple and Jain temple etc.

PARAMBIKULAM WILDLIFE SANC.: This excellent sanctuary is home to species like gaur (bison), sambar, spotted deer, Nilgiri langur, lion tailed macaque, sloth bear etc. Best Season- Feb. - April.

POTHUNDY : Popular picnic site.

SILENT VALLEY NATIONAL PARK : It is located in perhaps the last substantial stretch of evergreen rain forests in India. The key fauna includes, elephant, tiger, lion tailed macaque etc. Best season - Sept. - Mar.

SIRUVANI : Reservoir, Tribal life.

THENARI : Sree Rama temple, Sacred spring.

THIRUVALATHOOR : Ancient shrine known for exquisite woodwork and sculptures.

THRITHALA : Famous for monuments and historic ruins. Siva temple, Kattilmadam temple.

ACCESSIBILITY

By Air : The nearest airport for Palakkad is at Coimbatore (55 kms.) in Tamil Nadu and Kochi (160 kms.) in Kerala.

By Rail : Palakkad Junction is a major railhead of South.

By Road : The district is well connected by road.

IMPORTANT DISTANCES FROM PALAKKAD

Alappuzha	185	Kollam	280	Parambikulam	135
Alattur	24	Kottayam	196	Sabarimala	264
Changanassery	219	Kozhikode	119	Silent Valley N.P	80
Chittur	15	Malampuzha	12	Shoranur	40
Guruvayur	86	Malappuram	80	Sultan's Bathery	238
Kannur	209	Meenkara	32	Thalassery	186
Kasargod	275	Munnar	221	Thiruvananthapuram	351
Kalpetta	182	Nelliampathi	32	Thrissur	61
Kochi	135	Painavu	174		

PALAKKAD DISTRICT

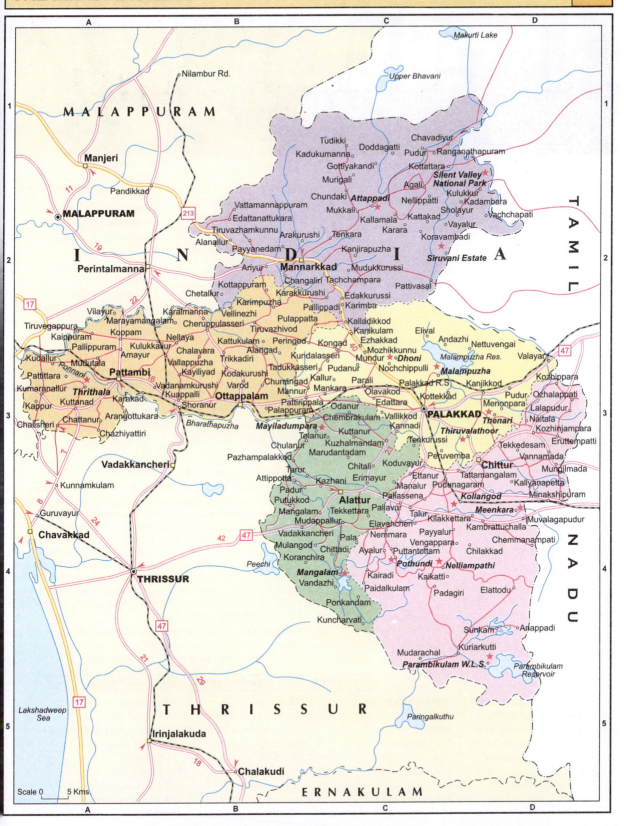

Welcome to... PATHANAMTHITTA DISTRICT

Gold plated shrine at Sabarimala

Lord Ayyappa

Pathanamthitta district popularly referred as the 'Headquarters of Pilgrimage Tourism' of Kerala or the 'Land of Temples' was carved out of Idukki, Alappuzha and Kollam districts in 1982. The district is close to the Western Ghats and is endowed with scenic landscape comprising of low undulating hills, extensive stretches of lush forests, rivers and charming countryside. It is also known for exuberant fairs and festivals which provide an insight into the rich cultural traditions of the region.

The district is considered to be industrially backward, but some traditional industries have been thriving here since early times. Thiruvalla taluk is known for its cane and rattan work industry. Copra is produced and exported from the district in large scale. Other important cash crops produced here are pepper, tapioca and rubber.

GENERAL INFORMATION

Area	: 1,475 sq. kms.
Population	: 1,231,577
Headqtrs.	: Pathanamthitta
Taluks	: 5
Blocks	: 9
Towns	: 4
Villages	: 68
Best Season	: Aug. - Mar.

PLACES OF INTEREST

ACHANKOVIL : Hindu pilgrim centre. The temple of Lord Dharmasastha here is said to be built by Lord Parasuram.

ARANMULA : The picturesque Hindu pilgrim centre is famous for the temple of Lord Krishna and the Aranmula Vallamkali (Boat Race), held during Onam festival.

CHARALKUNNU : Picturesque hill resort.

KONNI : Lush meadows, hills and plantations of clove and pepper. Wild elephants are also tamed here.

KOZHENCHERY : Trading centre and flourishing market for agricultural goods.

Maramon Convention - The annual Christian religious convention is held at Maramon in Mallapuzhasseri village near Kozhenchery in Feb. / Mar. It is believed to be the largest religious congregation of the Christians in Asia.

Niranam - The church here is the oldest in India and is said to be built by Saint Thomas, the Apostle in 52 AD.

MANNADI : Centre for Kerala Institute of Folklore & Folk Arts. Ancient Bhagavathi temple with fine sculptures. The annual festival at the temple is held in the month of Feb. / Mar.

NILACKAL : Ancient Siva temple, Estate of Farming Corporation and the Ecumenical centre of Christians.

PATHANAMTHITTA : Number of churches, temples and mosques built in close proximity. The Chandanakudam festival held at the mosque in the centre of the town is quite famous. **Omallur** (5 km.) - Rakthakanta Swamy Temple, Cattle fair.

Malyalapuzha (8 km.) - Bhagvathy Temple, Wall paintings.

Kadamanitta (8 km.) - Kadamanitta Devi Temple.

PERUNTHENARUVI : Spectacular waterfalls plunge down into a ravine from a height of about 60 - 100 ft.

SABARIMALA : The sacred 'Abode of Lord Ayyappa' is one of the most important Hindu pilgrim centre in the country. The holy shrine is located amidst dense forests in the rugged terrains of Western Ghats. Millions of pilgrims assemble here during the festivals of Vishu Vilakku (Apr.), Mandalapooja (Nov.- Dec.) and 'Makaravilakku' (mid Jan.), coinciding with Sankramam. The traditional route to Sabarimala is from Erumeli (40 kms.). Other routes are from Vandiperiyar, Uppupara and Chalakkayam via Plappally. These routes are famous for there scenic splendour and mythological value. Vehicular traffic is only upto Pamba, located 5 kms. from the holy shrine.

THIRUVALLA : Headquarters of the Malankara Marthoma Syrian Church. The Sree Vallabha temple here is known for the Kathakali dance performance as ritual offering everyday.

ACCESSIBILITY

By Air : Nearest airport from Pathanamthitta is at Kochi.
By Rail : Nearest railhead is at Thiruvalla. Kottayam is the main rail head for Sabarimala.
By Road : Pathanamthitta is well connected by road.

IMPORTANT DISTANCES FROM PATHANAMTHITTA & PAMBA

Pathanamthitta to...					
Chengannur	28	Sabarimala	72	Kannur	486
Konni	11	Thiruvalla	30	Kodungalor	275
Kozhenchery	13	Thiruvananthapuram	119	Kottayam (via Manimala)	116
Maniyar	20	**Pamba to...**		Kozhikode	388
Moozhiyar	57	Adoor	81	Ochira	116
Pamba	65	Alappuzha	137	Palakkad	330
Perunthenaruvi	36	Chengannur	93	Thiruvalla	102
		Guruvayur	288	Thiruvananthapuram	180

PATHANAMTHITTA DISTRICT

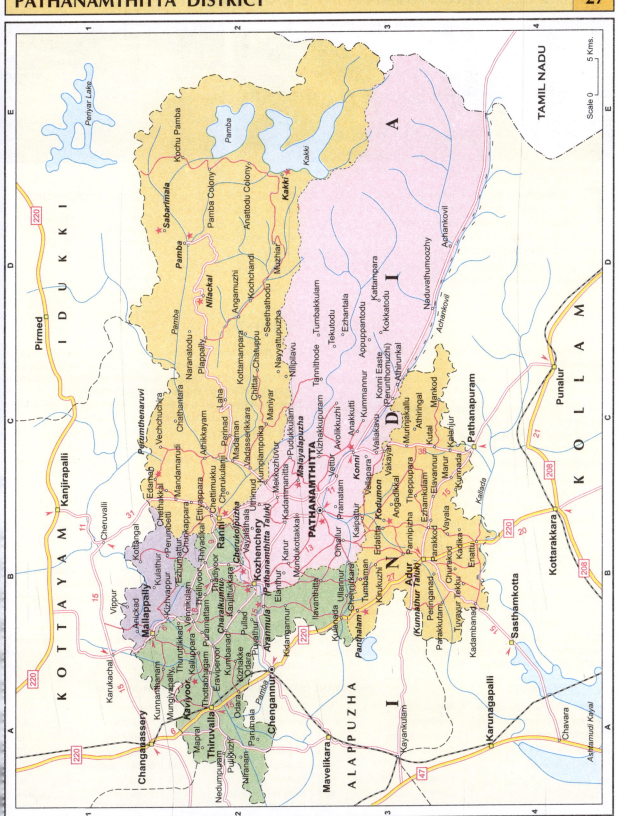

Welcome to... THIRUVANANTHAPURAM DISTRICT

Sree Ananthapadmanabhaswamy Temple

Govt. Art or Napier Museum

Kovalam Beach

Thiruvananthapuram, the southernmost district of Kerala is flanked by Western Ghats in the east and 78 kms. of flat coastal strip in the west. The beautiful land is a veritable paradise for the tourist. The wooded highlands of Western Ghats are dotted with excellent picnic spots. The long shoreline is peppered with silvery beaches of international repute. The backwater stretches of the district are truly amazing.

Thiruvananthapuram district is also noted for its rich history and culture. Magnificent monuments and ancient shrines attract tourists from all over.

GENERAL INFORMATION

Area	: 2,192 sq. kms.
Population	: 3,234,707
Headqtrs.	: Thiruvananthapuram
Taluks	: 4
Blocks	: 10
Towns	: 5
Villages	: 93
Best Season	: Sept. - May.

PLACES OF INTEREST

ANCHUTENGU : Beach, Relics of the fort and flagstaff, Tombs of Dutch and British.

ARUVIKARA : Ancient Bhagavathi temple on the banks of Karamana river.

KOVALAM : One of the finest beach resort of the world. Health and Yoga Centre.

NEYYAR DAM & WILDLIFE SANC. : Boating, Lion Safari Park, Crocodile Farm and Rich variety of birds and animals.

PONMUDI : Idyllic health resort known for its bracing climate, tea plantations, scenic splendour and hiking and trekking trails.

THIRUVANANTHAPURAM : Clean and beautiful capital city sprawling over seven low coastal hills.

Sri Ananthapadmanabha Swamy Temple - It is the most conspicuous landmark of the city. Lord Vishnu is represented as Sri Padmanabhaswamy or "lotus navel" and is depicted reclining on the coil of Sri Anantha, the sacred snake. The temple is a fine example of Kerala and Dravidian architecture and was rebuilt by Raja Marthanda Varma in 1733.

Kuthiramalika (Puthen Malika) Palace Museum - It is housed in a majestic palace built in traditional Travancore style and provides a rare insight into the lives of Travancore royalty.

CVN Kalari Sangham - Involved in the preservation of Kalarippayattu, an ancient martial tradition of the State. Provides Kerala's ayurvedic treatments.

Govt. Art (Napier) Museum - The museum building is built in traditional Kerala architecture with influences of Chinese and Mughal styles. Fine collection of bronzes, ornaments, costumes, masks, ivory carvings and musical instruments etc.

Zoological Gardens - It is one of the oldest and best zoo in India and is also regarded as the best laid-out zoo in Asia.

Govt. Observatory - It is one of the oldest observatory in the country. Panoramic view of the city and surroundings.

Science & Technology Museum & Priyadarshini Planetarium - Complete insight into the achievements of India in the fields of science and technology.

Chacha Nehru Childrens' Museum - It has a rich collection of over 2000 dolls, stamps, masks and paintings etc.

Akkulam Lake & Boat Club - Boating, Largest childrens' park in Kerala.

Veli Tourist Village - Picnic spot and Waterfront park.

Shankhumugham Beach : Beautiful beach, Recreation club, the Matsya Kanyaka sculpture & Children traffic training park.

Vettukad or 'Madre de Deus' Church (7 kms.) - Popular among people of all faiths.

Beema Palli (5 kms.) - Important Muslim pilgrim site.

VARKALA : Sree Janardhana Swami Temple (one of the seven most important Vaishnavite shrines), Sivagiri Mutt, Beach and Nature care centre.

ACCESSIBILITY

By Air : Thiruvananthapuram has an international and domestic airport.

By Rail : Connected by major cities of the country.

By Road : Excellent road network.

IMPORTANT DISTANCES FROM THIRUVANANTHAPURAM

Alappuzha	160	Kollam	71	Palakkad	351
Aruvikara	16	Kottayam	148	Ponmudi	61
Changanassery	130	Kovalam	12	Sabarimala	136
Guruvayur	296	Kozhikode	382	Shoranur	322
Kannur	465	Malappuram	366	Sultan's Bathery	502
Kasargod	560	Munnar	304	Varkala	40
Kalpetta	467	Neyyar Dam & Sanc.	32	Thalassery	471
Kochi	220	Painavu	215	Thrissur	299

THIRUVANANTHAPURAM DISTRICT

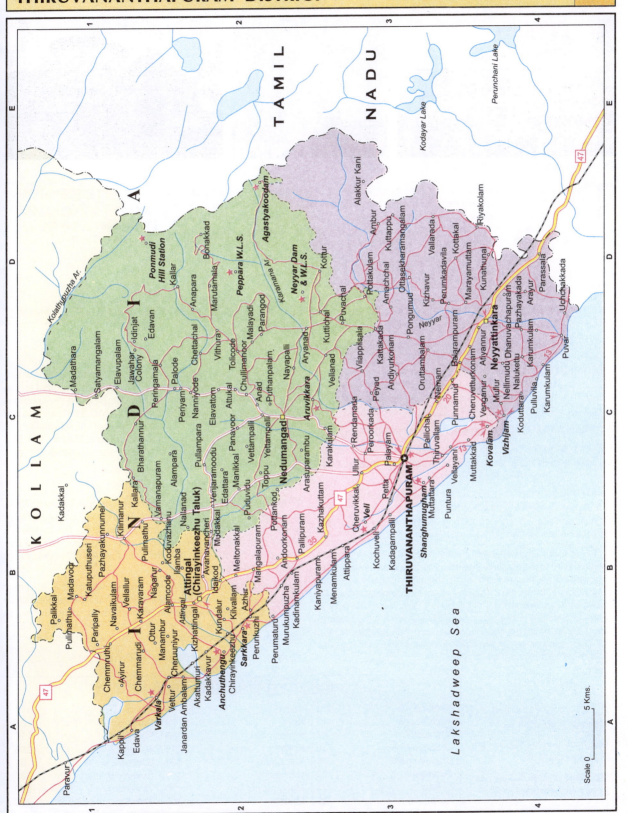

Welcome to... THRISSUR DISTRICT

Pooram Festival, Thrissur

Church, Thrissur

Avittathur Shiva Temple Near Thrissur

Thrissur district has played an important role in the political history of the Kerala state as well as the entire southern India. It is also referred as the 'Cultural Capital' of Kerala, due to its rich cultural heritage and archaeological wealth. The district has some of the most important temples, churches and mosques. Its colourful festivals like Pooram at Thrissur, Ekadasi at Gurvayur and Bharani at Kodungallor display the rich cultural traditions of the land.

The district is also endowed with splendid scenic beauty. The waterfalls at Athirampally and Vazhachal are among the best seen in Kerala. Seventy five percent of the total geographical area is under cultivation. The important crops grown are paddy, coconut, tapioca, arecanut, cashew, banana, rubber, pepper, turmeric, pulses etc. Various traditional industries like handloom, weaving, oil crushing, pottery, coir, basket making, bell metal, mat weaving, etc. flourish in the district.

GENERAL INFORMATION

Area	: 3,032 sq. kms.
Population	: 2,97,5,440
Headqtrs.	: Thrissur
Taluks	: 5
Blocks	: 17
Towns	: 40
Villages	: 209
Best Season	: Sept. - Mar.

PLACES OF INTEREST

ARATTUPUZHA : Famous for Arattupuzha Pooram festival, held in Mar. / Apr. The deities of 46 temples from the neighbourhood villages are brought at night in colourful processions to the local temple of Lord Sastha.

ATHIRAPPILY FALLS : 80 ft. high waterfall, Scenic site.

CHALAKUDI : Historical town and important 'timber centre'. It was the base of Tipu Sultan during the attack on the 'Travancore Lines', known as Krishnakotta or Nedumkotta.

CHERUTHURUTHI : Famous for Kerala Kalamandalam, established by poet Sri Vallathol Narayana Menon in 1930. The institute imparts training in various traditional art forms like Kathakali, Mohiniyattam, Thullai and folk dances.

GURUVAYUR : The 'Dwarka of South', one of the most important pilgrim centre of Kerala. Sree Krishna Swamy temple is said to be created by Guru, the perceptor of the *Devas* and *Vayu*, the Lord of Winds. Lord Krishna, the presiding deity of the temple is popularly known as "Guruvayurappan" or the Lord of Guruvayur. The temple is also known for the healing powers. This is also a good place to watch Kerala Hindu marriage ceremony and *'Annaprasanam'*, the first feeding ceremony of the child. *Ekadasi* (Nov. / Dec.) is the most important festival of the temple.

KODUNGALLOR : Ancient centre of trade and commerce and described as the 'first emporium in India'. First settlement for the Jews, Christians and Muslims in India. St. Thomas, the Apostle is said to have first landed at Muziris port in 52 AD. The town also has the first mosque in India. The striking feature of the mosque is that it faces east unlike other mosques which face Mecca. It is also known for the Kurumba Bhagavathi temple and its Bharani Festival in Mar.- Apr.

PEECHI DAM : Picnic site, Boating, Gardens.

THRISSUR : The 'Cultural Capital' of Kerala is built around a hillock, crowned by the famous Vadakkumnathan (Siva) Temple, believed to have been founded by legendary Parasurama. The temple is a classical example of Kerala style of architecture and houses several sacred shrines. It is believed that Adi Shankaracharya spent his last days here.

Pooram Festival (Apr. - May), well known for the 'Elephant umbrella' competition is the major attraction of Thrissur. Beautifully decorated elephants with ceremonial umbrellas carry the deity on a chariot around the main temple. Other places of interest are - Archaeological Museum, Zoo, Fort, Palace and Churches etc.

VAZHACHAL : Picturesque waterfall, Dense forests.

ACCESSIBILITY

By Air : Nearest airport for Thrissur is at Kochi.

By Rail : Thrissur is an important rail head.

By Road : The district has good road network..

IMPORTANT DISTANCES FROM THRISSUR

Alappuzha	130	Kalpetta	196	Painavu	113
Arattupuzha	12	Kochi	79	Palakkad	61
Athirappily	63	Kodungallor	50	Peechi Dam	20
Changanassery	158	Kollam	219	Sabarimalai	203
Cherutharuthi	35	Kottayam	135	Shoranur	32
Guruvayur	25	Kozhikode	134	Sultan's Bathery	209
Kannur	223	Malappuram	95	Thalassery	200
Kasargod	289	Munnar	160	Thiruvananthapuram	299

THRISSUR DISTRICT

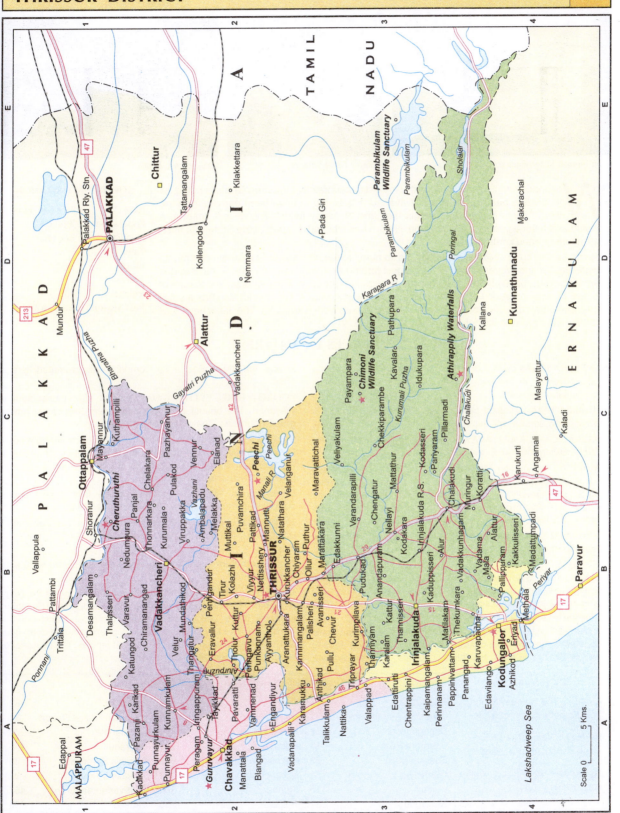

Welcome to... WAYANAD DISTRICT

Jain Temple, Sultan Battery

Malabar Giant Squirrel

Valliyoorkav Temple

Wayanad district nestled amidst the majestic mountains of Western Ghats is noted for its pristine beauty. The name Wayanad is believed to have been derived from the word 'Vayalnadu', which means the 'land of paddy fields'. The district is set in a peculiar and unique geographical position. Nature has blessed this part of the State with mist-clad mountains and verdant valleys.

The rich cash crop plantations of pepper, cardamom, coffee, tea, spices and other condiments has perhaps made Wayanad one of the biggest foreign exchange earner in the State. Besides plantation crops, paddy is the most important agriculture produce. The characteristic feature of the district is the presence of large number of tribals or *Adivasis*. The district also has a small Jain community consisting of Gounders, who came here from Karnataka. The Jains have built beautiful temples in the district.

GENERAL INFORMATION

Area	: 2,131 sq. kms.
Population	: 7,86,627
Headqtrs.	: Kalpetta
Taluks	: 3
Blocks	: NA
Towns	: 1
Villages	: 48
Best Season	: Aug. - May.

PLACES OF INTEREST

BANASURA SAGAR DAM : Largest earth dam in India. The islands at the reservoir in the backdrop of Banasura hills provide a spectacular scenic view.

CHEMBRA PEAK : Highest peak in the district and a 'trekker's paradise'. Breathtaking scenic beauty.

EDAKKAL CAVE, AMBALAVAYAL : Magnificent rock caves pre-historic carvings on the rock wall.

KALPETTA : Famous for Mahaveera shrine, one of the few Jain shrines of Kerala and Maidani Mosque. There are many important Jain temples around the town which are - Ananthanatha Swami Temple at Puliyarmala ; Glass Temple of Koottamunda and Santhinatha Temple at Venniyod.

KURUVA ISLAND : Excellent picnic spot located amidst tributaries of east flowing Kabbani river. The island has rare species of birds, orchids and herbs.

Lakkidi : The 'Gateway to Wayanad' is located 5 kms. south of Vayittiri. It is one of the highest location in the district and commands a picturesque scenery. The 12 kms. long journey from Adivaram to Lakkidi is a fascinating experience.

PAZHASSI TOURIST RESORT, MANANTHAVADI : Ideal picnic spot, Fine aquarium, Coin operated toys for children and Boating facilities. Pazhassi Raja, the 'Lion of Kerala', who waged war against the British East India Company was cremated here in 1805.

POOKOT LAKE, VYTTIRI : Most sought after tourist spot in Wayanad. The beautiful natural fresh water lake is set amidst green mountains. Boating facility is also available.

SULTAN'S BATHERY : The hill station and historical centre is noted for a fort built by Tipu Sultan in the 18th century. The famous Panamarram fort here played an important role during the Pazhassi Rebellion.

Chethalayam Waterfall - The beautiful falls amidst scenic surroundings are just 12 kms. from Sulthan's Battery.

THIRUNELLI : Famous for the temple referred as 'Thekkan Kasi'. It is believed that a dip in the holy water of 'Papanasini' will wipe off all sins.

Pakshipathalam - The famous bird watching centre is 10 kms. from Thirunelli.

WAYANAD WILDLIFE SANC. : It is an integral part of the Nilgiri Biosphere Reserve and borders the famous Mudumalai Sanctuary in Tamil Nadu and Nagarhole and Bandipur Sanctuaries in Karnataka. The key fauna includes elephant, spotted deer, gaur, sloth bear and a large variety of birds and reptiles. The best season is from December to April.

ACCESSIBILITY

By Air : The nearest airport from Kalpetta is at Kozhikode.

By Rail : Nearest rail heads are at Kannur and Kozhikode.

By Road : Kalpetta is well connected by road.

IMPORTANT DISTANCES FROM KALPETTA

Alappuzha	307	Kochi	251	Palakkad	182
Banasura Sagar Dam	21	Kollam	396	Pazhassi Tourist Resort	34
Changanassery	335	Kottamunda	20	Sabarimala	385
Chembra Peak	15	Kottayam	211	Shoranur	156
Edakkal Cave	25	Kozhikode	63	Sultan's Bathery	35
Guruvayur	171	Malappuram	98	Thalassery	92
Kannur	115	Munnar	350	Thiruvananthapuram	467
Kasargod	181	Painavu	350	Thrissur	196

WAYANAD DISTRICT

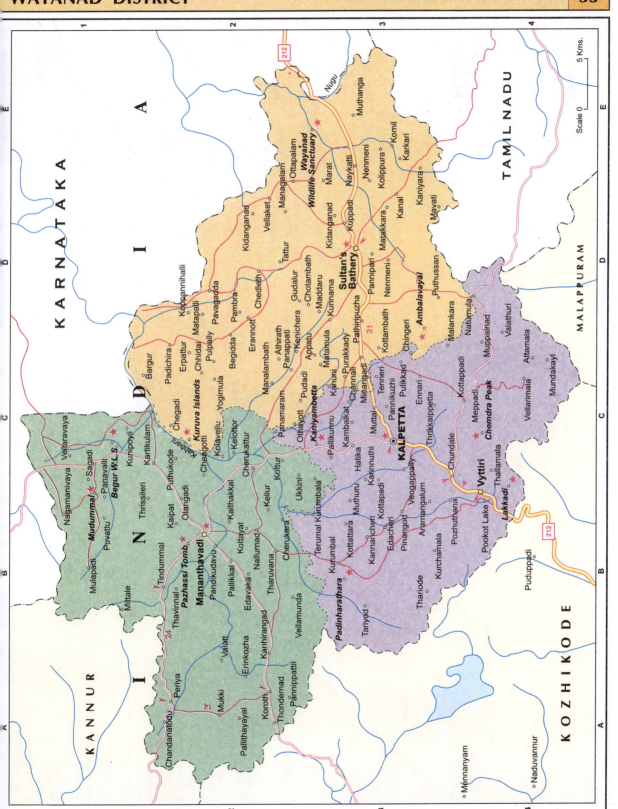

THIRUVANANTHAPURAM CITY

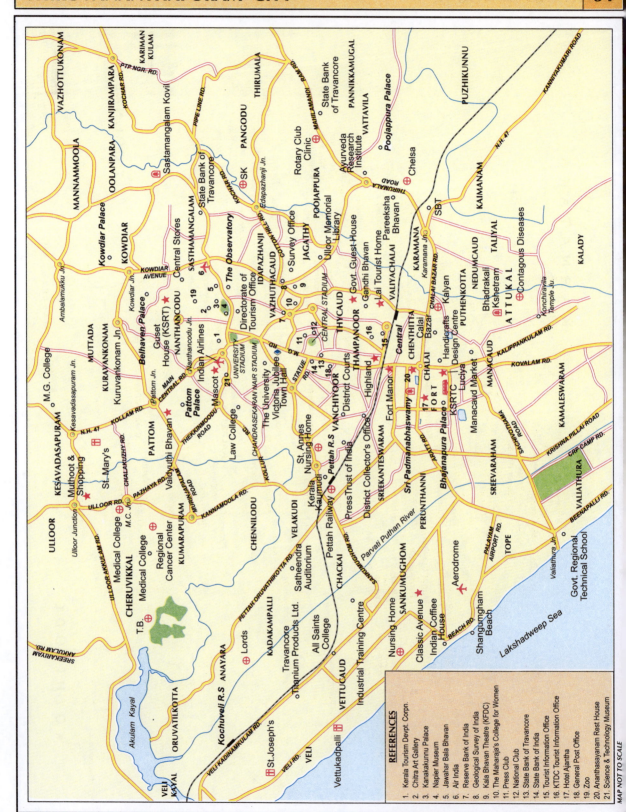

THIRUVANANTHAPURAM - MG ROAD AREA

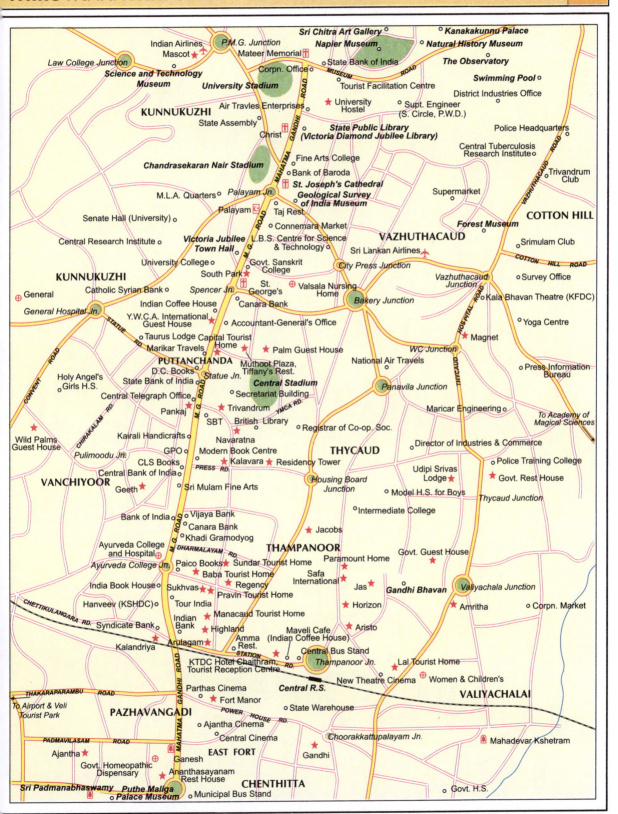

KOCHI CITY 36

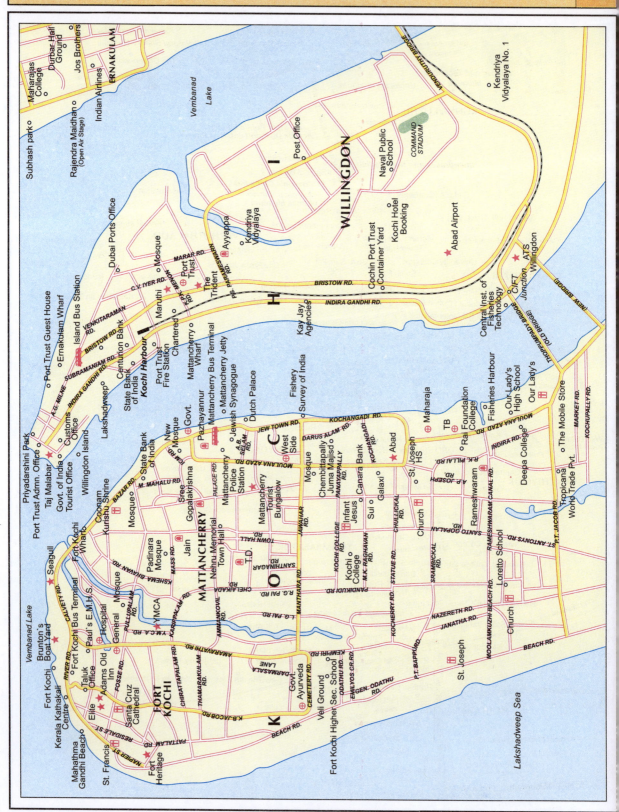

ALAPPUZHA CITY

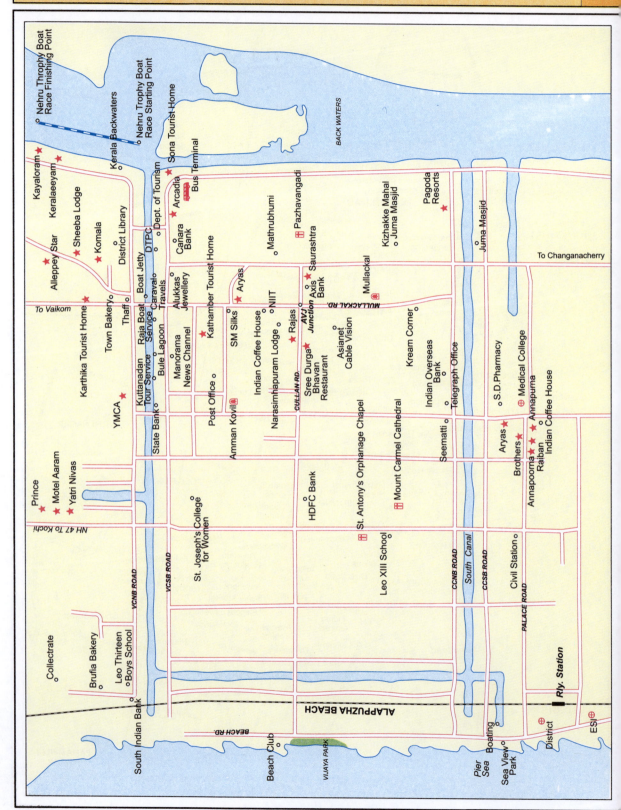

KOVALAM

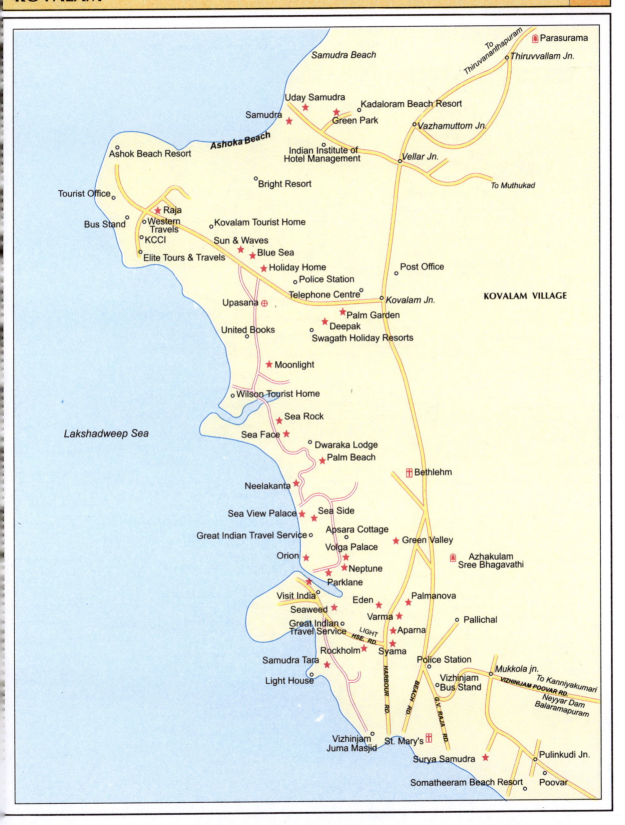

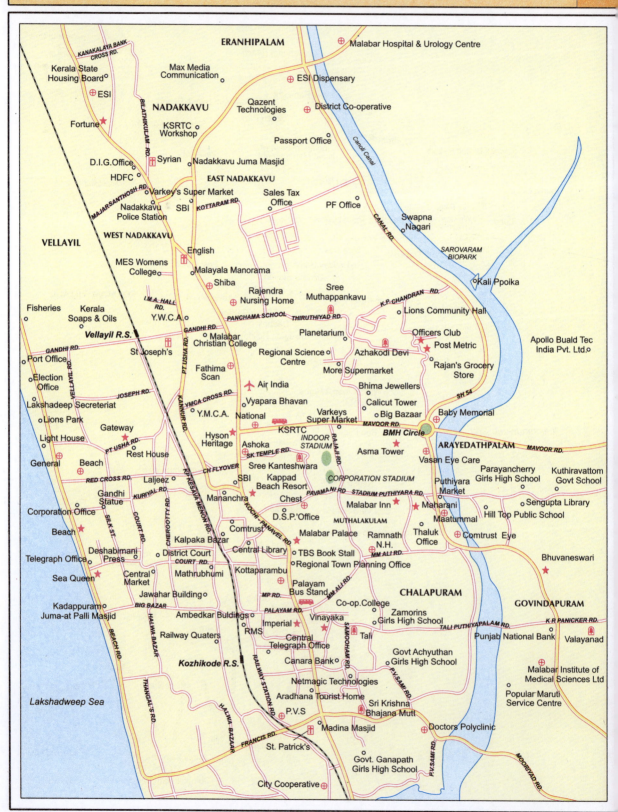

KOTTAYAM CITY & PALAKKAD CITY

KOTTAYAM CITY
NOT TO SCALE

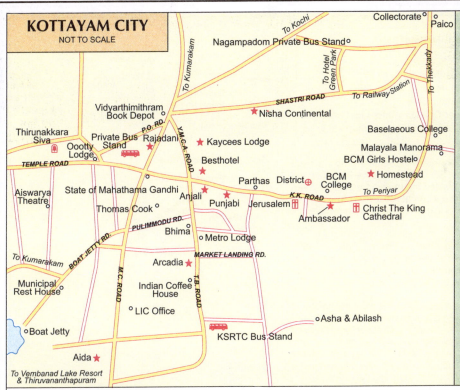

Kottayam, the beautiful backwater town is set in the foot hills of verdant Western Ghats. The town is surrounded by fertile landscape and most attractive scenery.

It is an important trading centre for cash crops like rubber, tea, pepper and cardamom and is one of the most prosperous part of the state.

Kottayam, the land of literacy, latex and lagoons is the first totally literate town of India. It is also the headquarters of Malyalam Manorma, India's second largest daily newspaper in terms of circulation.

The town is strategically located and well connected by rail and road.

PALAKKAD CITY
NOT TO SCALE

Palakkad is located 79 kms. from Thrissur, on the Coimbatore - Thrissur highway and is a major railway junction of the State. The nearest airport is at Coimbatore, 55 kms. away.

Palakkad derives its name from *Pala* (Alsteria Scholaris) tree and *Kadu* (forest), as it is said that the area was full of *Pala* trees. The small town is the centre of a large rice growing region.

The places of interest in the town are -

The Fort, built by Hyder Ali of Mysore in 1776.

The famous **Kalpathy Siva Temple** located on the banks of river Kalpathy. The annual car festival of the temple is held in November attracting large number of devotees from all over the State.

Palakkad is also a good base to visit the famous Parambikulam Wildlife Sanctuary (135 kms. via Pollachi) and Silent Valley National Park in Kundai Hills, 80 kms. from here.

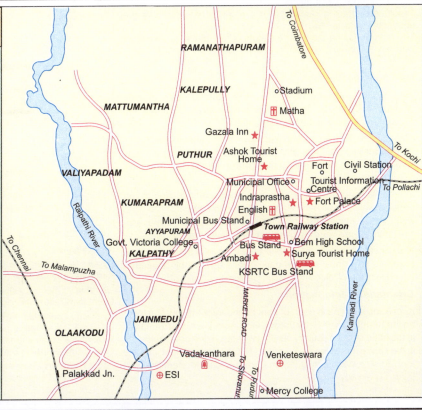

PERIYAR NATIONAL PARK

42

GENERAL INFORMATION

Area	:	777 sq. km.
Temperature	:	Summer Max. 29°C 18°C
		Winter Max. 21°C Min. 16°C
Annual Rainfall	:	2,600 mm.
Clothing	:	Summer-Cottons Winter-Light woolen
Season	:	Dec. May Best Season : Mar. - May

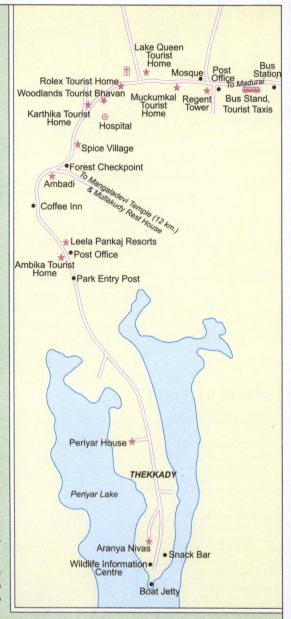

Periyar National Park at Thekkady is Southern India's most popular wildlife sanctuary. Set on the attractive lake side, the 777 sq. km. sanctuary was created by the old Travancore State Government in 1934. The park encompasses a 26 sq. km. artificial lake, built by the British in 1895 to provide water to the temple city of Madurai in Tamil Nadu.

The sanctuary was designated a part of *'Project Tiger'*, in 1973, and offers a fairly good chance of seeing the majestic Indian Tiger in its natural habitat. It is also acclaimed to be the best place in the world for studying all the aspects of elephantine life.

Besides tigers and elephants, the sanctuary is a natural habitat to wide variety of wildlife including bison, sambar, wild boar, spotted deer, leopards, jungle cats, rare species of Malabar flying squirrel, stripe necked mongoose, black Nilgiri langurs and monkeys etc. There are plenty of water fowl which perch on the dead trees in the lake. Woodland birds, owls and hornbills can also be seen in the forest.
Picturesque Periyar National Park is also known for its scenic beauty and bracing climate. It is a pleasant escape from the rigours of day to day life.
The boat cruise on the serene waters of the lake is an excellent way to watch the wildlife and the pristine beauty of the park.

Watching the Wildlife

The chances of viewing the wildlife are best during the hot months of March and April, as the water holes in the forest dry up forcing the animals to come to the lake for a drink.

Boat trips on the lake are the usual way of touring the sanctuary. The standard two-hour boat trips are arranged in the large KTDC craft and Forest Department craft. Boats of varied sizes on charter hire are also available.

There are special viewing platforms which can be used if you prefer to walk with a Game Ranger. The visitors are not allowed to walk in the jungle without a guide. Elephant rides are also available, but are more for fun rather than viewing the wildlife.

The third and best way is to spend a night in one of the observation towers or rest houses in the park. These have to be booked in advance at the Wildlife Information Centre.

Orientation & Information

Kumily located on the north of park boundary is the junction town on the Kerala / Tamil Nadu border. 4km. from Thekkady, Kumily is in the heart of spice country bustling with spice dealers. *Thekkady*, is the centre inside the park where KTDC hotels and boat jetty are located. The Wildlife Information Centre is located near the boat jetty in Thekkady.

Accessibility

By Air : Nearest airport is at Madurai (140 km.) in Tamil Nadu and Kochi (208 km.) in Kerala.

By Rail : Nearest railhead is at Kottayam (110 km.) on the Ernakulam - Thiruvananthapuram line.

By Road : Connected by bus services from Thiruvananthapuram (271 km.), Kochi (185km.), Kottayam (110 km.) and Madurai (140 km.). All the buses originating or terminating at Periyar start and finish at Aranya Nivas in Thekkady. The buses also stop at Kumily.

Local Transport - Buses and autos are available. Cycles can be rented at KTDC Periyar house and Aranya Nivas.

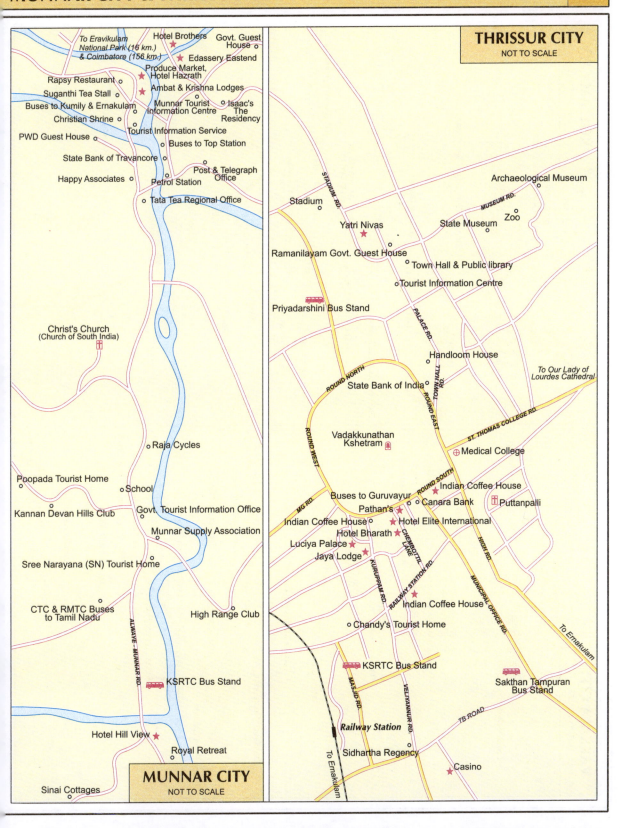

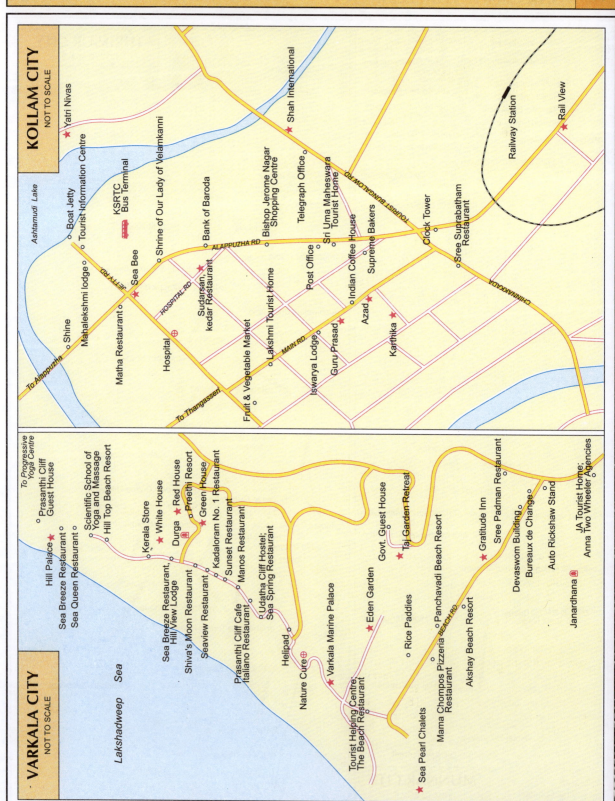

LAKSHADWEEP

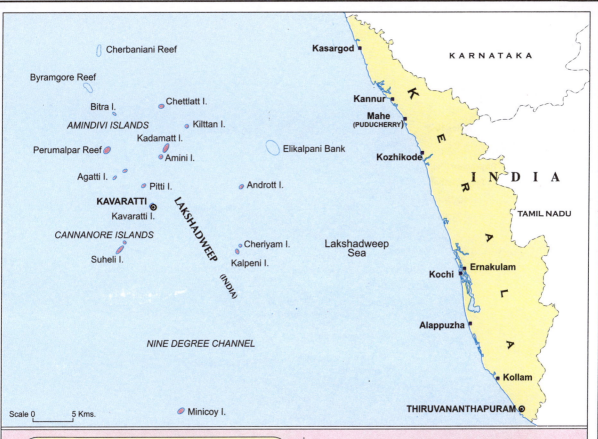

GENERAL INFORMATION
Capital : Kavaratti   **Area** : 32 sq. km.
Population : 60,595   **Languages** : Makatakam & Mahi
Temperature : *Summer* Mean Max. 35°C Mean Min. 22°C
                 Winter Mean Max. 32°C Mean Max. 20°C
Famous For : Beautiful beaches, diving and snorkelling
Best Season : October to April

LAKSHADWEEP AT A GLANCE

Island	Area (sq. km.)	Population	Famous for
Agatti	2.71	5667	Beautiful Lagoons, corals and multicoloured fish
Amini	2.59	6445	Handicrafts made of tortoise shell and coconut shell, Stone carvers, Folk songs
Andrott	4.84	9119	Jumma Mosque, tomb of Arab Apostle Ubaidulla, Finest Coconuts of the islands
Bangaram *	0.58	61	One of the finest tourist spots in the country
Bitra	0.10	225	Sea birds, Turtles and fishes
Chettlatt	1.04	2050	Handicraft industry and tombs
Kadamatt	3.13	3983	Building stones and coir
Kalapeni	2.28	4079	Huge storm bank of coral debris
Kavaratti	3.63	8664	Beautiful lagoons, Mosques
Kittan	1.63	3075	Traditional folk songs & dances
Minicoy	4.37	8313	Southernmost island, Tuna finshig centre, Lighthouse
Pitti			Bird Sanctuary

* *Bangaram is 'inhabited' only by the staff of the tourist resort*

Lovely Lakshadweep island, set in the lap of Arabian Sea, has of 36 charming islands, of which only 10 are inhabited. Lakshadweep is the smallest Union Territory of India in terms of population and area. But if we sum up the entire lagoon area of 42,00 sq. kms., 20,000 sq. kms. of territorial waters and 7,00,000 sq. kms. of economic zone, Lakshadweep stands out to be one of the largest territories of India. Ethnically, the people of the island are very similar to the people of Kerala. Sunni Muslims are in majority over here. They are very conservative and adhere to their customs and traditions.

The island are believed to be formed by coral activity. The reefs make these island unique in colour and tranquility. Lakshadweep is also a paradise for the diving enthusiasts. The islands are 220 to 440 km. away from Kochi in Kerala. These can be approached by air or ship from Kochi. Lakshadweep has an aerodrome at Agatti island.

MAJOR ROUTES FROM THIRUVANANTHAPURAM

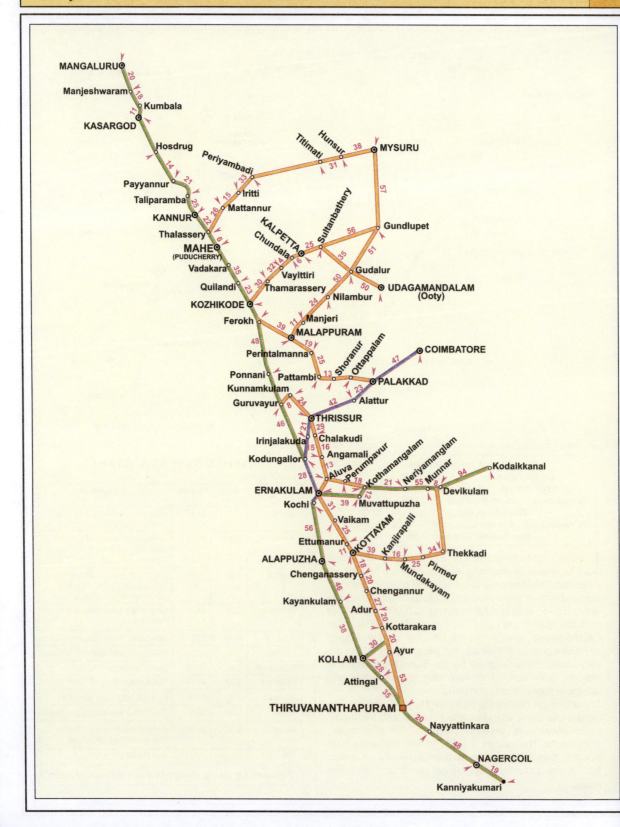

KERALA - Distance Guide (All distances in km.)

47

KOCHI to...		KOZHIKODE to...		THIRUVANANTHAPURAM to..		THRISSUR to...	
Agartala	4040	Agartala	3912	Agartala	4064	Agartala	4011
Agra	2391	Agra	2213	Agra	2611	Agra	2312
Ahmadabad	1881	Ahmadabad	1687	Ahmadabad	2040	Ahmadabad	1831
Aizawl	3965	Aizawl	3841	Aizawl	3988	Aizawl	3878
Ajmer	2407	Ajmer	2213	Ajmer	2566	Ajmer	2357
Akola	1594	Akola	1416	Akola	1754	Akola	1516
Aligarh	2474	Aligarh	2296	Aligarh	2694	Aligarh	2395
Allahabad	2187	Allahabad	2009	Allahabad	2407	Allahabad	2108
Ambala	2785	Ambala	2607	Ambala	3005	Ambala	2706
Amritsar	3040	Amritsar	2862	Amritsar	3260	Amritsar	2961
Asansol	2492	Asansol	2368	Asansol	2516	Asansol	2413
Aurangabad	1393	Aurangabad	1212	Aurangabad	1613	Aurangabad	1314
Bengaluru	533	Bengaluru	355	Bengaluru	753	Bengaluru	454
Barauni	2632	Barauni	2454	Barauni	2840	Barauni	2553
Barddhaman	2407	Barddhamn	2283	Barddhaman	2431	Barddhaman	2328
Bareilly	2603	Bareilly	2430	Bareilly	2823	Bareilly	2524
Belagaavi	885	Belagaavi	662	Belagaavi	1044	Belagaavi	806
Ballari	828	Ballari	605	Ballari	1048	Ballari	749
Bhagalpur	2720	Bhagalpur	2578	Bhagalpur	2744	Bhagalpur	2641
Bhavnagar	2068	Bhavnagar	1874	Bhavnagar	2227	Bhavnagar	2018
Bhopal	1981	Bhopal	1756	Bhopal	2154	Bhopal	1855
Bhubaneshwar	1919	Bhubaneshwar	1795	Bhubaneshwar	1943	Bhubaneshwar	1840
Bikaner	2640	Bikaner	2446	Bikaner	2799	Bikaner	2590
Bilaspur	1971	Bilaspur	1793	Bilaspur	2191	Bilaspur	1892
Chandigarh	2831	Chandigarh	2653	Chandigarh	3051	Chandigarh	2752
Chennai	684	Chennai	686	Chennai	708	Chennai	605
Chitradurga	690	Chitradurga	467	Chitradurga	910	Chitradurga	611
Coimbatore	193	Coimbatore	186	Coimbatore	413	Coimbatore	114
Cuttack	1944	Cuttack	1820	Cuttack	1968	Cuttack	1865
Dehra Dun	2772	Dehra Dun	2594	Dehra Dun	2992	Dehra Dun	2693
Delhi	2594	Delhi	2416	Delhi	2814	Delhi	2515
Dhanbad	2469	Dhanbad	2345	Dhanbad	2493	Dhanbad	2390
Dindigul	316	Dindigul	339	Dindigul	330	Dindigul	237
Gangtok	3041	Gangtok	2917	Gangtok	3065	Gangtok	2962
Gaya	2536	Gaya	2358	Gaya	2717	Gaya	2457
Guwahati	3402	Guwahati	3278	Guwahati	3426	Guwahati	3323
Gwalior	2281	Gwalior	2100	Gwalior	2501	Gwalior	2202
Hyderabad	1095	Hyderabad	917	Hyderabad	1315	Hyderabad	1016
Imphal	3886	Imphal	3762	Imphal	3910	Imphal	3807
Indore	1795	Indore	1614	Indore	1990	Indore	1752
Jaipur	2442	Jaipur	2261	Jaipur	2697	Jaipur	2439
Jaisalmer	2476	Jaisalmer	2282	Jaisalmer	2635	Jaisalmer	2426
Jalandhar	2957	Jalandhar	2779	Jalandhar	3177	Jalandhar	2878
Jammu	3176	Jammu	2998	Jammu	3396	Jammu	3097
Jodhpur	2320	Jodhpur	2126	Jodhpur	2479	Jodhpur	2270
Kandla	2246	Kandla	2052	Kandla	2405	Kandla	2196
Kanniyakumari	307	Kanniyakumari	488	Kanniyakumari	87	Kanniyakumari	386
Kanpur	2390	Kanpur	2212	Kanpur	2610	Kanpur	2311
Kohima	3741	Kohima	3617	Kohima	3765	Kohima	3662
Kolhapur	988	Kolhapur	765	Kolhapur	1147	Kolhapur	909
Kolkata	2360	Kolkata	2236	Kolkata	2384	Kolkata	2281
Lucknow	2461	Lucknow	2283	Lucknow	2681	Lucknow	2382
Ludhiana	2898	Ludhiana	2720	Ludhiana	3118	Ludhiana	2819
Madurai	270	Madurai	405	Madurai	264	Madurai	303
Mangaluru	447	Mangaluru	224	Mangaluru	606	Mangaluru	368
Mumbai	1384	Mumbai	1212	Mumbai	1543	Mumbai	1356
Mysuru	397	Mysuru	216	Mysuru	598	Mysuru	318
Nagpur	1582	Nagpur	1404	Nagpur	1786	Nagpur	1506
Panaji	842	Panaji	619	Panaji	1001	Panaji	721
Patna	2521	Patna	2343	Patna	2725	Patna	2445
Puducherry	591	Puducherry	557	Puducherry	605	Puducherry	485
Porbandar	2275	Porbandar	2081	Porbandar	2434	Porbanda	r2225
Pune	1221	Pune	998	Pune	1380	Pune	1144
Rajkot	2097	Rajkot	1903	Rajkot	2256	Rajkot	2047
Rameswaram	442	Rameswaram	577	Rameswaram	401	Rameswaram	470
Salem	358	Salem	351	Salem	565	Salem	279
Shillong	3502	Shillong	3378	Shillong	3526	Shillong	3423
Shimla	2936	Shimla	2758	Shimla	3156	Shimla	2857
Srinagar	3469	Srinagar	3297	Srinagar	3689	Srinagar	3390
Thanjavur	449	Thanjavur	445	Thanjavur	523	Thanjavur	370
Tiruchchirappalli	395	Tiruchchirappalli	391	Tiruchchirappalli	469	Tiruchchirappalli	316
Tirunelveli	256	Tirunelveli	559	Tirunelveli	172	Tirunelveli	457
Tirupati	730	Tirupati	602	Tirupati	922	Tirupati	651
Tuticorin	304	Tuticorin	540	Tuticorin	220	Tuticorin	438
Udaipur	2133	Udaipur	1939	Udaipur	2292	Udaipur	2083
Vadodara	1768	Vadodara	1574	Vadodara	1927	Vadodara	1718
Varanasi	2312	Varanasi	2134	Varanasi	2516	Varanasi	2236
Vijayawada	1112	Vijayawada	988	Vijayawada	1136	Vijayawada	1033
Vishakhapatnam	1494	Vishakhapatnam	1370	Vishakhapatnam	1518	Vishakhapatnam	1415
Warangal	1235	Warangal	1057	Warangal	1455	Warangal	1156

KERALA - FAIRS, FESTIVALS & INDEX

KERALA - FAIRS & FESTIVALS

MONTH	FAIR / FESTIVAL	VENUE	SPECIAL FEATURE
January / February	Makara Vilakku	Sabarimala	
	Great Elephant March (17th - 20th Jan.)	Thrissur and Thriuvananthapuram	Colourful procession of elephants
	Village Fair (3rd Jan.)	Near Kovalam	It is a recreation of the rural Kerala
February / March	Utram Festival	Tripunittura	
	Sivaratri	Aluva, Tripunittura	Special Poojas and cultural events
	Flavour & Nishagandhi Dance Festival	Thriuvananthapuram	Delicious Indian cuisine available
March / April	Kodiyettu	Guruvayur	
	Ashtami Festival & Elephant Races	Guruvayur	Elephant processions and races
April / May	Pooram	Thrissur, Arattupuzha	Elephant umbrella competition
	Vishu Vilakku	Sabarimala and Kannur	Prayers and lighting of lamps
May / June	Sankaracharya Jayanthi	Kaladi	Birth anniversary of Adi Sankracharya
June / July	Boat Races and Processions	Ambalapuzha	Spectacular boat racing
July / August	Nehru Trophy Boat Race	Alappuzha	World famous Snake Boat Racing
August / September	Onam & Tourism Week Celebrations	Throughout Kerala	Most important festival of Kerala
	Boat Races	Alappuzha, Aranmula, Kumarakom etc.	Boat racing events
September / October	Krishna Jayanthi	Guruvayur	Lord Krishna's birth anniversary
	Mahanavami	Thiruvananthapuram	
October / November	Mandalam Festival	Sabarimala	
	Ashtami	Vaikam	Elephant processions, dances & music
November / December	Mandala Pooja	Sabarimala	
	Ekadasi Festival	Guruvayur	Fasting and devotional exercises
	Sivagiri Festival	Varkala	
	Christmas	All over the State	Major Christian festival

INDEX OF IMPORTANT PLACES

Adur . . . . 27 B 3	Ezhimala . . . . 13 A 2	Kozhikode . . . . 21 B 4	Painavu . . . . 11 B 3	Silent Valley . . . . 25 D 2
Agali . . . . 25 C 2	Guruvayur . . . . 31 A 2	Kumarakom . . . . 19 A 3	Pala . . . . 19 C 2	Sultan's Bathery . . . . 33 D 3
Alappuzha . . . . 7 B 3	Haripad . . . . 7 B 4	Kundara . . . . 17 B 3	Palakkad . . . . 25 C 3	Takazhi . . . . 7 B 4
Alattur . . . . 25 C 4	Hosdrug . . . . 15 B 4	Kuriarkutti . . . . 25 D 5	Pallippuram . . . . 25 A 3	Talipparamba . . . . . . 13 B 2
Aluva . . . . 9 B 2	Idukki . . . . 11 B 3	Lahai . . . . 27 C 2	Palluruthy . . . . 9 B 3	Thangasseri . . . . 17 A 3
Ambalapuzha . . . . 7 B 4	Irinjalakuda . . . . 31 B 3	Mahe (Puducherry) . . 13 C 4	Pappinisseri . . . . 13 B 3	Tannirmukkam . . . . . 19 A 3
Ambalavayal . . . . 33 D 3	Kaladi . . . . 9 C 2	Mala . . . . 31 B 4	Parambikolam . . . . . 25 D 5	Thalassery . . . . 13 C 4
Ana Mudi . . . . 11 C 1	Kalarkod . . . . 7 B 3	Malampuzha . . . . . . 25 D 3	Parassala . . . . 29 D 4	Thekkadi . . . . 11 C 4
Aralam WLS . . . . . . 13 D 3	Kallar . . . . 29 D 2	Malappuram . . . . 23 B 3	Paravur . . . . 9 A 2	Thenmala . . . . 17 D 2
Aranmula . . . . 27 B 2	Kalpetta . . . . 33 C 3	Malayattur . . . . 9 C 1	Paravur . . . . 17 B 4	Thiruvalla . . . . 27 A 2
Arattungal . . . . 7 B 2	Kanayannur . . . . 9 B 4	Mallappally . . . . 27 B 1	Parssinikadavu . . . . . 13 B 2	Thiruvananthapuram . 29 C 3
Arppukara . . . . 19 B 3	Kanichukulangara . . . 7 B 2	Mananthavadi . . . . . 33 B 2	Pathanamthitta . . . . 27 B 3	Thrissur . . . . 31 B 2
Aruvikara . . . . 29 C 3	Kanjirapalli . . . . 19 D 3	Manjeri . . . . 23 B 3	Pattambi . . . . 25 A 3	Tikkodi . . . . 21 A 3
Attappadi . . . . 25 C 2	Kannur . . . . 13 B 3	Manjeshwara . . . . . . 15 A 1	Pathanapuram . . . . . 17 C 2	Tirur . . . . 23 A 4
Attingal . . . . 29 B 2	Kappad . . . . 21 B 4	Mannarashala . . . . . . 7 B 4	Payyoli . . . . 21 A 3	Tiruvambadi . . . . 21 D 3
Bekal . . . . 15 B 3	Karunagapalli . . . . . . 17 A 2	Mannarkkad . . . . 25 C 2	Perintalmanna . . . . . 23 C 4	Todupuzha . . . . 11 A 3
Beypore . . . . 21 B 5	Kasargod . . . . 15 A 3	Mattancheri . . . . 9 A 3	Periyar NP & WLS . . 11 C 4	Tottapalli . . . . 7 B 4
Bharanikavu . . . . 7 C 5	Kavaratti 45	Mattupatti . . . . 11 C 2	Peroorkada . . . . 29 C 3	Tripunittura . . . . 9 B 3
Chalakudy . . . . 31 B 3	Kayamkulam . . . . 7 C 5	Mavelikara . . . . 7 C 5	Perumbavur . . . . 9 C 2	Udumbanchola . . . . . 11 C 3
Changanassery . . . . 19 B 4	Kochi . . . . 9 A 3	Moncombu . . . . 7 B 3	Pirmed . . . . 19 C 1	Uzhavur . . . . 19 C 1
Chavakkad . . . . 31 A 2	Kodungallor . . . . 31 B 4	Mundakkayam . . . . . 19 E 3	Pon Mudi . . . . 11 C 2	Vadakara . . . . 21 A 2
Chavara . . . . 17 A 2	Kollam . . . . 17 A 3	Munnar . . . . 11 C 2	Ponnani . . . . 23 A 5	Vadakkancheri . . . . . 31 B 2
Chengannur . . . . 7 C 4	Kollangod . . . . 25 C 4	Muvattupuzha . . . . . . 9 D 3	Punalur . . . . 17 C 2	Vadasserikara . . . . . 27 B 2
Cherthala . . . . 7 B 2	Kondotti . . . . 23 A 3	Narakal . . . . 9 A 2	Punnamada . . . . 7 B 3	Vaikam . . . . 19 A 2
Cheruthuruthi . . . . . . 31 B 1	Koni . . . . 27 C 3	Nedumangad . . . . . . 29 C 2	Punnapra . . . . 7 B 3	Vandiperiyar . . . . 11 C 4
Chittar . . . . 27 C 2	Kothamangalam . . . . . 9 D 2	Neyyar Dam & WLS . 29 D 2	Quilandi . . . . 21 B 3	Varkala . . . . 29 A 2
Chittur . . . . 25 D 3	Kottakkal . . . . 23 B 3	Neyyattinkara . . . . . . 29 C 4	Ranni . . . . 27 B 2	Vayalar . . . . 7 B 2
Devikulam . . . . 11 C 2	Kottarakkara . . . . . . 17 B 2	Nilambur . . . . 23 C 2	Sabarimala . . . . 27 E 1	Vayittiri . . . . 33 C 4
Ernakulam . . . . 9 B 3	Kottayam . . . . 19 B 3	Nileshwaram . . . . . . 15 B 4	Sasthamkotta . . . . . 17 B 2	Vellani . . . . 11 B 4
Erumeli . . . . 19 D 4	Kovalam . . . . 29 C 4	Ochira . . . . 17 A 1	Sholayur . . . . 25 D 2	Vizhijam . . . . 29 C 4
Ettumanur . . . . 19 B 2	Kozhenchery . . . . . . 27 B 2	Ottappalam . . . . 25 B 3	Shoranur . . . . 25 B 3	Wayanad WLS . . . . 33 E 3